GROW YOUR PRIVATE PRACTICE

Jane Travis

LEGAL NOTICES

No part of this publication may be reproduced or transmitted in any material form (including photocopying or storing in any medium by electronic means) without the written permission of the author Jane Travis.

The purpose of this book is to educate, entertain and provide information on the subject matter covered. All attempts have been made to verify the information at the time of publication, and the author does not assume any responsibility for errors, omissions or other interpretations of the subject matter. The purchaser or reader of this book assumes responsibility for the use of this material and information. The author assumes no responsibility or liability on behalf of any purchaser or reader of this book.

Copyright © 2019 Jane Travis

All rights reserved.

ISBN: 9781692305529

Dedications

To all the amazing counsellors that don't think they are. Because you are. Amazing, that is.

This book is also dedicated to my gorgeous sons, who are at the heart of everything I do and the reason I am able to follow my dreams.

What others are saying

This is an excellent book if you wish to grow your private practice. It is clear and concise and takes you through the whole process, so you will be organised, inspired, and ready to do business. I would certainly recommend Jane's book

Wow, what a great book to help sort out being in private practise! Clear and easy to read is what I love about this book. Packed with so many tools and worksheets. No excuses for not doing your marketing with this little helper by your side.

Such an informative and well set out book which has helped me what I needed to do and see where I was going off at tangents. Well worth the purchase.

Resources

You will find the link to Grow Your Private Practice and all of the book resources at the back of the book.

54 Specific Ways To Attract Therapy Clients

Follow this link and get your copy. www.janetravis.co.uk/attract-therapy-clients

Table Of Contents

Introduction	1
Part 1: Quickstart	13
Chapter 1 Be more swan	15
Chapter 2 How to get started when you don't know where to start	21
Chapter 3 Seedling niche	29
Chapter 4 Directories	37
Chapter 5 Putting down roots	41
Chapter 6 Networking	47
Part 2: Mindset	59
Chapter 7 Imposter Syndrome	61
Chapter 8 Overcome self sabotage	79
Chapter 9 Making peace with money	99
Chapter 10 The business of therapy	127
Chapter 11 Time for business?	137
Part 3: Practical	147
Chapter 12 Niche	149
Chapter 13 How to choose a niche	157
Chapter 14 Messaging	169
Chapter 15 The Empathy Exercise	181
Chapter 16 Websites	185
Chapter 17 Search engine optimisation (SEO)	203

Chapter 18 Content marketing	207
Chapter 19 Social media	221
Chapter 20 Advertising and offline marketing	237
Chapter 21 Your clients journey into therapy	247
Chapter 22 Turning your dreams into goals	255
Conclusion	263
Resources	267
About the author	269

INTRODUCTION

Therapy Rebrand

I'm Jane Travis, a counsellor since 2005, and I am on a mission to change the face of therapy. Together we're going to give therapy a rebrand and change the way people view our work. Let's shift the public perception of counselling and psychotherapy to benefit all - clients, ourselves and the communities around us.

Attitudes to counselling

I asked counsellors and psychotherapists in the Grow Your Private Practice Facebook group 'what reaction do you get when you tell people that you're a counsellor?'. Here are some of the replies:

- Ooh, don't analyse me!
- Don't you try your psychobabble nonsense with me
- So just a cup of tea and a chat then?
- Who needs a counsellor, I just talk to my friends
- I couldn't do that, listening to people moan all the time
- So, can you read my mind? What am I thinking now?

Introduction

- My mum doesn't believe in therapy
- My brother had counselling, and it made him worse
- You don't look like a counsellor
- So basically, you sit and ask how people feel
- Ooh, sorry for swearing!
- I'm having a problem with... (insert problem they want advice on here)
- Are you one of those airy-fairy hippie people?
- Don't you get fed up of listening to people whining on

Therapist Tip: If people think you're going to analyse them here are two things you could try saying:

- You'll know if I'm analysing you because I'll charge you
- I wasn't, but I am now!

Have you heard any of these? Have you ever *said* any of these? Have you ever wanted some counselling to look at an issue but for some reason you haven't gone ahead with it? Why was that? It's worth reflecting on, as it will give insight on why others may be putting it off.

Those examples above are fun, right? But there were also these responses:

- I get anything from intrigue to suspicion
- I just don't say what I do in social situations anymore
- People run away and hide because they think I'm psychoanalysing them
- Sometimes I feel nervous telling people what I do
- I find it a real conversation stopper
- People back away and find someone else to talk with

Introduction

Some of these responses were repeated by many people, which is worrying for two reasons:

- That people have such a negative response to counselling or counsellors
- That these responses are making us have fears about talking about what we do, which impacts on our ability to be visible and attract clients

What does this say about the public view of counselling?

- Therapy is treated with suspicion - don't analyse me
- We are undervalued - so basically you just say, 'how does that make you feel'?
- And it makes people feel awkward - sorry for swearing (like we're royalty)

The problem is if we feel awkward talking about therapy, the public will never understand what we do. That makes us feel undervalued, which stops us talking about what we do and creates a vicious circle. That's not going to do much for improving perceptions.

Counselling as a punishment

When visiting a friend, her daughter had been found to have committed some heinous crime (eating sweets, I think) and she was being told off in front of me, much to both mine and her daughter's embarrassment. After admonishing her for quite some time she said 'if this carries on you'll end up having to see someone like Jane', and this wasn't in a 'don't worry sweetie, we'll get you some help ' way, it was in a 'this is going to hurt' way. I thought, is this really how she sees me? Is this how people see us as counsellors?

Introduction

No wonder people are often terrified of therapy!

Some people think accessing counselling means:

- They are broken and need fixing
- They are stupid weak and silly
- They think we're going to judge them
- They think we're going to tell them what to do
- They think we will make them do something they don't want to
- They think counselling is a punishment for not getting 'it' right

What if private practice focused on prevention?

People associate counselling with mental health issues, but can you imagine how much better it would be for them to invest in some therapy before it got to the point of doctors visits and time off work? To get help when they first notice they have a low mood or are struggling with an aspect of their life or relationship rather than wait till they reach rock bottom? This isn't a new concept, I think many counsellors and psychotherapists want this. How can we make this happen?

People have no shame around getting coaching

On the contrary, it's seen as personal development, and people are proud of getting coaching, even boasting about it. Well counselling, is coaching with bells on. Business coaching to help improve your business because you love it and see it as important and worth spending time and money on. That's seen as positive. Life coaching shows you value yourself and want to improve your life which is seen as positive too. What if visiting a counsellor to

Introduction

help improve the quality of your life and relationships, and increase your self-acceptance was seen as extremely positive too?

What if counselling was the best self-care you could give yourself?

The client's relationship with a therapist is one of the rare times in life someone is on your side 100%. No judgement, no advice or telling what to do, no hidden agenda. Just 100% focus on the clients and their needs. How wonderful does that sound?

So how can we convey that message to the public? How can we let them know who we help, what we help with, and how they will feel? That we are there for them, work hard to truly understand them and be 100% on their side? Well, we'll be exploring these questions in this book.

Part of being a private practitioner is spreading the word that counselling helps address many issues and can help people:

- Feel more comfortable asking for needs to be met
- Be able to say no to unwanted requests
- Feel less anxious in social situations
- Sleep better
- Stop self-harming
- Not be haunted by guilt and shame
- Drop coping mechanisms that no longer help

Because if you don't, they will move on and find someone that does.

Fear

I remember the very first time I went for counselling back in my early twenties. I was terrified, I knew I needed help but had

Introduction

literally no idea what to expect. There weren't so many counsellors around then, and I found the details of someone local. She was psychodynamic, which couldn't have been more terrifying to me. I had to lay on a couch while she sat just behind me so I couldn't see her. I thought our sessions were being filmed or recorded in some way, I've no idea where that idea came from, but it was there. I barely said anything, and as a psychodynamic therapist, neither did she. I'd listen to the clock tick loudly and watched the hands barely move as time slowed to a crawl. Then I paid my hard-earned cash and slunk away, admonishing myself for not saying anything. Stupid stupid stupid!

People get scared about going to therapy. They are going to talk about their most raw, painful memories, their embarrassing or shameful stories, they are going to lay themselves open to a stranger, and their only experience of this previously may have ended in ridicule. So yes, there's fear and a lot of it. It's our job, as private practitioners to take away some of that fear, and we do that in the way we communicate with them and everything we do.

Mental health

In the UK, counselling is available for free on the National Health Service via your GP. Recently a lot of work has gone into raising awareness of mental health issues which is valuable and important work. But now that people's awareness has been raised, what will they do?

Counselling is accessed via your GP, and you go to your GP when you are ill. Therefore, counselling is for those people with mental illnesses and most people don't identify with having a mental illness. This means they don't get the help they need and

Introduction

feel increasingly worse until it *does* become a mental health issue when they do have to visit their GP.

People access counselling for many reasons, not just a mental health crisis. Things like the breakdown of relationships, bereavement, low self-esteem, stress and work-life balance, to name a few. So, if they are feeling:

- Lonely
- Anxious
- Worthless
- Struggling to communicate with their partners
- Consumed by grief - which people understand if it's a partner or a parent, but what if it's grief for a much-loved pet or even a celebrity?

Then they tell themselves not to be so silly, that they're just being weak, they should pull themselves together or that no one else feels like this. Many think they've done something wrong or failed in some way to be in a situation where they need this type of help. They may feel that this proves that they aren't strong enough, or simply aren't good enough.

Maybe you've had a client apologising for wasting your time because they should be happy, as they have a house or a job etc., and then go on to tell you about years of neglect, sadness, loneliness, feeling worthless or abuse. Or clients that apologise for being there because they feel sure there are other people that need help more than they do and then go on to share a similar horror story.

If the perception is that going to counselling is a punishment or shameful, means they have failed or makes them feel they have

Introduction

to go and stand in front of the headmistress and be made to feel small because of their misdemeanours, they will run for the hills.

If people, and by people, I mean your potential clients, think counselling is a punishment, why would they spend their hard-earned money to access it? They know they will have to face painful stuff, so why would they put themselves through that?

Mixed messages

We get very mixed messages as therapists. On the one hand, we are told that counselling is important, transformational, life-changing and even life-saving, which it is. On many TV shows, there are resident therapists to help callers and guests with any issues that come up, and the answer to virtually any problem is to see a counsellor.

There's a perception that within six sessions, we'll be able to fix any problems or issues that people have. It seems we are miracle workers!

On the other hand, we're told that there's no money available to fund it so you can't have a salaried job. God forbid we get paid to do this much needed vital work. Our many, varied and hard-worked for qualifications now aren't enough, so we are expected to jump through increasingly smaller hoops that get set on fire.

Organisations and charities sometimes take advantage of our generous nature and desire to help people, which we find hard to stand up to.

How are therapists portrayed in the media?

Well, there's Frasier, a popular show but let's face it, he's a pious

Introduction

snob who's not really relatable and certainly not like any of the wonderful therapists I know. Often therapists are portrayed writing on a notepad as someone lays on a couch. Or increasingly, we are seeing 'bad' therapists on TV are highly ineffectual and unethical with no boundaries and no idea about confidentiality. Again that's not like any of the counsellors I've ever met.

Given that many people seem to be afraid of us and our alleged 'magical powers', I think it's time for a rebrand because the therapists I know are just people - warm, friendly, compassionate, accepting and pretty damned wonderful people, actually!

The relationship

The clients' relationship with the therapist is one of the rare times in life someone is on your side 100%. There's no judgement, no unasked for advice, no being told what to do, no one 'competing' with you (you know the type, you have a headache, they have a migraine!) or just waiting for you to stop talking so they can talk about themselves. Basically, no hidden agenda, ever.

It doesn't sound like punishment

How can we convey this message to the public? How can we let them know who we help, what we help with, and what results they can expect if they take action?

But I can't promise results!

No, quite rightly you cannot and should not be promising potential clients results, that would be unethical. However, you can and should let them know you can help them, otherwise, why would they bother? We talk more about this in chapter 14 on messaging.

Introduction

People want a solution to their problem

No one ever wants to feel like they need counselling, so it's our job to convey the benefits to clients and let people know we can help. We have to let them know that they can expect to:

- Feel more comfortable asking for needs to be met
- Be able to say no to unwanted requests
- Feel less anxious in social situations
- Sleep better
- Feel more confident
- Stop self-harming
- Not be haunted by guilt and shame
- Understand themselves
- Recognise self-sabotaging behaviour
- Drop coping mechanisms that no longer help

Because if you don't let them know you can help, they will move on and find someone else that does.

Ultimate self-care

As private practitioners, it's our job to help change these attitudes towards therapy. It helps the public, it helps the NHS, it helps communities, it helps individuals, and it helps us. Let's talk about therapy being the **best ever** quality of self-care that you can give yourself, that therapy is about prevention and by accessing it when you first notice yourself struggling, you can prevent it from becoming more serious.

We can convey this message through everything we do. So, when someone at a party says, 'don't analyse me', instead of

10

Introduction

feeling awkward, come back with 'Oh, I don't do that, I just help people to have more fulfilling lives'. Doesn't that feel better?

We can convey this message through the social media posts that we write, the blogs and other content that we produce and through everything we say and do. Let's make our message 'counselling is the best gift you can ever give yourself'. Let's take away the shame around therapy and make people proud to be looking after themselves. Let's raise the profile of counselling.

Are you going to join the Therapy Rebrand movement?

PART 1: QUICKSTART

CHAPTER 1 BE MORE SWAN

Swans are beautiful birds, aren't they? Beautiful - and BIG!

Have you ever seen a swan take off? If you have, you'll know it takes a whole lot of effort - did I mention they are a BIG bird!? First, they have to paddle hard with their feet and flap their wings to raise their big body above the water. Then, they run on top of the water for a good while. Then they start flapping their wings like crazy to get some lift before they get to the right velocity and start to become airborne. Then there's more hard work to get some height until eventually, the whole process becomes easier, their large wings beat, and they fly and glide gracefully. They are in flow.

It's exactly like that when marketing your private practice.

Getting started is the most labour-intensive part: there's a lot to do, a lot of moving parts, a lot of things to get started and a lot to learn. For most people, running a private practice is a whole new skill set, and if you've never run a business before it can be confusing and overwhelming. Even if you have been involved in running a business before, running a private practice has its own considerations, like ethics, personal disclosure and confidentiality.

It takes time, a lot of time at the outset. Time to figure out your niche, what you want on your website, your branding, what type of content marketing (blogging, video blog, podcast, workshops) to use, which social media platform is right for you. Then to learn the skills and use your marketing to attract clients

Yes. Overwhelming.

However, the good news is you don't have to do them all, and you don't have to have all your ducks (or swans) in a row before starting. In fact, I'm going to show you how to get started when you don't know where to start so you can attract and work with clients to bring in some income even if you are on a very tight budget. Yes, even without a website.

The four stages of competence

You may have looked at the four stages of competence in your training.

Unconscious incompetence: You don't know how to do something but aren't aware of this. An example would be writing a blog. You start with no awareness of why you might need to, or how to go about doing it.

Conscious incompetence: You understand that writing blogs will attract clients and is a great marketing tool, while also being very helpful for people. You see how it will be beneficial, but you're aware that you've no idea how to go about it. So, you take a beginner blogging course.

Conscious competence: You learn how to write blogs, but it takes a lot of concentration, maybe checking notes frequently. It takes a lot of time.

Unconscious competence: You've written blogs for a while and have become familiar with it, so can get into the flow without having to think. It's now second nature.

It's important to know that with everything in life, we go through these four stages. So why would business be any different? It's going to feel difficult, confusing and overwhelming - there's no other way. This is where we sometimes fall down because we expect too much of ourselves. We expect it to be easy, to just put ourselves in an online directory or pay for an ad and clients will turn up. We forget to factor in the time and effort it takes to get started and learn new skills.

Most often the skills aren't overly hard, they're just new, and it will take some time to get to the 'unconscious competence' stage. But you will.

You don't have to do ALL THE THINGS straight away, but you do have to commit to working on your business because otherwise, you won't get the clients, money and success you want. If you want a successful private practice, you have to remember what it is - a business and businesses take time, money and effort to be successful.

Running a business can be hard work. It takes persistence and consistency, time and effort. If you're not okay with prioritising your business and ultimately, you're not ready to put in the effort required, maybe you're not okay with running a business at this time: maybe you're better with a job. That's okay, being self-employed isn't for everyone, so it's best to explore this before you start, and save yourself some heartache. Harsh? Maybe, but I'm just being truthful, because if you don't feel passionate about being a therapist and about seeing those transformations, then it's going to be hard to muster up the motivation to do the work, prioritise marketing and go through the trial and error that's involved.

However, once you've done the heavy lifting of getting started, things change. You know what you're doing. You have systems in place and know the steps you need to take to do your marketing. It all becomes easier and less time consuming, and as you start seeing results, getting clients and getting the income you want or need. You start believing in yourself and trust the process. Now your confidence grows as your business grows.

That swan starts to soar with grace and ease. That initial investment in time, money and effort starts to pay off. You have a regular routine to marketing your practice knowing what you need to do and doing it in the most effective way possible with new clients regularly calling.

What can I say - it's totally worth it, so go easy on yourself. Be gentle because getting started with something new takes energy and time.

Are you ready to embark on this fantastic adventure? Then let's get started.

Activity: Growth Journal

Have you ever bumped into a friend you haven't seen for a while and their child seems to have grown enormously, and you say the thing you hated hearing as a child, namely 'ooh, haven't they grown?!'

Be More Swan

The parent doesn't notice it because the change is so gradual, but because you only see them sporadically, you notice the massive changes as they move from baby to toddler to child to teen to adult.

This is what happens with your practice. Your practice is your baby, and because you are with it every day you won't necessarily see the changes and progress both it, and you have undergone. You're too close.

I invite you to start a Growth Journal. This will be a journal for your practice, and you get to record not only your progress but also your struggles, successes, fears, failures, and sabotages.

This is useful for many different reasons:

- When you go through a difficult period, as you inevitably will, you'll have written proof of how far you've come
- You can record all your successes, no matter how small
- You can spot patterns and so protect yourself from self-sabotage

I suggest getting a luxurious journal or notebook in order to do this and make the process positive and uplifting, which will encourage you to make this a habit. But you could also use a low cost, simple notebook, a 'page a day' diary or set something up online. There are any number of free journaling apps to try but find whatever feels right for you because it's only useful if you actually use it.

Your mission, should you choose to accept it, is to set up a Growth Journal.

Your Growth Journal: Questions for reflection

- Your first entry in your Growth Journal is 'How do I feel about starting this Growth Journal?'
- Where are you in the four stages of skills learning?

CHAPTER 2 HOW TO GET STARTED WHEN YOU DON'T KNOW WHERE TO START

I'm writing this book by drawing on my experience, which, in most cases, means learning from my mistakes.

In my experience, many people starting out (yes, myself included) get caught up in doing the fun, sexy things we think a business should do, like get a logo or business cards. Well, I say, don't. As a therapist just starting out, you need to allow yourself some breathing space to allow your practice to form, and find some answers to questions like:

- Who am I as a therapist?
- What issues do I want to work with?
- Who are my ideal clients?
- What do I want from my practice?

We look at all these things later in this book, but if you try and force it now, you will likely feel dissatisfied in a few months' time. It's far better to allow yourself some time and space to find your way. But while you give yourself time and start working out what's right for you going forward, you can still be working with clients and bringing in an income.

For this reason, it's not worth spending a huge amount of time, money and effort on things like logos, business cards and even websites at this point - there is time for that in the future. What you like now, you'll probably hate in 6 months' time. It happens to us all.

Beating perfectionism and procrastination

I see many people waiting until they have everything ready before they start taking clients. They want the perfect website, perfect branding, perfect pictures, logos, leaflets, business cards etc. But if you wait until everything is perfect, you'll be waiting forever. It's classic perfectionism and procrastination sabotaging you. The longer you wait, the more those fears marinade and the more your inner critic will have a chance to bully you, and your Imposter Syndrome will whisper lies to you.

You will make mistakes whether you start now or in a years time, but if you start now, a year from now you'll have waded through the most tricky part of getting started and have a whole year of experience under your belt. We'll be taking a closer look at these things later in the book, but for now, all you need to know is if you wait for things to be perfect, you'll never start.

This is the mantra of this book: Start where you are, use what you have and upgrade when you can.

Perfection is simply not necessary. In fact, striving for perfection will hold you back. Let's look at how you can get started while working it all out. This way, you'll start earning money which you can then re-invest into something that will benefit your practice in the future, like a website.

Self-awareness

I'm sure I don't need to tell you how important self-awareness is in life, and it's also important in business because how you do life is how you do business. If you are a cautious person, you will be the same in business. If you are an introvert, extrovert, risk-taker, dreamer or fearful, then you will be in that in business too. The trick is to use this to your advantage and work to your strengths. This could mean if you are an extrovert, you'll probably enjoy networking, or if you are an introvert, maybe blogging would be more your style. There are many ways to market your practice and attract clients, and all of them work, so take some time working out what's best for you, because if you enjoy your marketing, then you're halfway there.

What are your processes? Are you someone that likes to take their time and thoroughly research new things before you get started (people might tell you that you overthink), or maybe you are a jump first look later person? Again, knowing which you are will help you and ease stress. If you're someone that likes a deep understanding before getting started, you need to factor this into your learning time, and if you just get stuck in, then you will need to factor in 'tweaking' time later to learn more detail.

What motivates you? Is it money, taking on challenges, making a difference, being creative, feeling valued, learning new skills that stretch you, a need for security, status, rewards? Because if you know what motivates you, you can use this to your advantage by seeking out what you need or setting motivational goals.

Think of your practice as a beautiful jacket you are having specially tailored for you.

Time management

I'm willing to bet that you're a busy person. My money is pretty safe to be honest because we're ALL busy these days, so how can you find the time to do all the things needed to grow your private practice? Well, I've got your back because, throughout this book, I shall be encouraging you to use The Pomodoro Technique.

What is The Pomodoro Technique?

The Pomodoro Technique is a simple yet effective productivity technique that uses a timer. Francesco Cirillo, the person who created this technique, called it "The Pomodoro Technique" because it started with him using a tomato-shaped kitchen timer to help him study in college. (Pomodoro is "tomato" in Italian.) I love it, because of its simplicity, and if I'm struggling with procrastination, perfectionism or having an uninspired day, it never fails to spark me into action. Before we get into the how, here is why it's such an effective method:

There are frequent breaks

This is important, as it keeps the body and brain refreshed.

Focus on one thing

Multi-tasking is vastly overrated! It's proven to reduce productivity because each time you switch activity, your brain has to remember where you were and what you needed to do. It blocks your flow and can take up to 10 minutes to get back up

How To Get Started

to speed with what you were doing. Imagine writing a blog - you get creative, your brain is focussing on the subject matter, and you are in your flow. Then you get the ping of an email notification so stop what you're doing to read and deal with that. When you come back to your blog, it takes time and mental energy to get back into that creative space.

Feel good factor

Each time you complete a Pomodoro, give yourself a little reward and allow yourself to feel that satisfaction.

Ditch the overwhelm

In life and business, there is always more to do, and there always will be. With this method, you know after a set amount of time you can stop. That feels manageable.

Time boundaries

According to Parkinson's Law, work expands to fill the time we make available. If you give yourself a month to complete something, it will take a month, but give yourself a day it'll take a day. We know this to be true as every year here in the UK we have between April and the following January to complete tax returns, yet every year millions of people are frantically completing their returns in the last 2 weeks of January.

Challenge

Working against the clock can feel like a fun challenge to get as much done in the allotted time as possible, and a great sense of achievement.

Using the Pomodoro Technique

Decide what to do, and make it an actual, tangible thing that can

How To Get Started

be finished. Pick a SMART goal, where you choose goals that are:

- Specific
- Measurable
- Achievable
- Relevant
- Timely

'Start writing a blog post', isn't a good goal as it doesn't have a specific outcome, and if there is no outcome, you won't know when you have finished. If you don't know when you've finished, you will never get that 'yay, I just did the thing!' payoff. Make it 'write an outline of a blog post' which is specific, and you'll definitely know when you've finished it. Make it specific, measurable and achievable in the time you have. To make this more effective:

- Turn off all distractions - Facebook, phone etc.
- Set your timer for 25 minutes and work on that one thing
- When the timer goes off, set the timer for 5 mins and take a break. Walk around your garden, get a drink, stretch, do some desk yoga. But move
- When the timer goes off, repeat the process and start working again
- After four Pomodoro's, take a longer break of 15-20 minutes

There are many Pomodoro apps you can buy, and I've used a couple, now I just use the timer on my phone. It's simple and free, just the way I like it.

I use a form of The Pomodoro Technique in other ways too. When it comes to things like brainstorming, researching, mindmapping, planning etc. I use one short burst of say 10 minutes and get as much done as I can, and when the timer goes off, I stop.

It's so easy to get caught up in a social media rabbit hole, so give yourself ten minutes twice a day to check your social media and respond to any comments etc.

Work on accepting that done is better than perfect. 80% is good enough. Do the task and then move on as progress always trumps perfection.

I am aware of my procrastination habits, so last year my word of the year was 'FOCUS'. I focussed on one thing at a time and got serious about removing distractions. Guess what? My business grew, and yours can too.

The Pomodoro Technique helps you focus on each task so your productivity will increase, and you achieve more in less time, meaning you can achieve more and then get on with your life. We'll take a deep dive into time management in chapter 12 too, but for now, start using The Pomodoro Technique, it's a little miracle!

Activity: Practice The Pomodoro Technique

Take something from your to-do list that you have been putting off, set a timer and concentrate on doing it until the timer goes off.

Your Growth Journal: Questions for reflection

- Knowing that we'll be focusing on progress not perfection, what comes up for you?
- Are you a hare - rushing ahead, moving quickly, or a tortoise - plodding, methodical, slow and steady? What are the 'pros' and 'cons' for you, and how can you take advantage of the 'pros', and protect yourself from the 'cons'?

CHAPTER 3 SEEDLING NICHE

Having a niche is one of the foundations to grow a strong private practice on, and is about understanding your audience and connecting with them. You may already know with who or what issues you want to work with, in which case you won't need a Seedling Niche, you can go straight into using that niche to attract clients.

If you don't have a niche, I invite you to choose a very broad one, which we'll call your 'Seedling Niche'.

When you first start thinking of a niche, you need to go through a process of defining:

- What it is that you love
- What you are good at
- What the world needs and
- What you can be paid for

As you get clearer about this, your Seedling Niche will develop and start to put roots down and spreading its branches out to

Seedling Niche

get a feel for what is going to create the best environment for you to work in. Then you can branch out, pruning ideas and then adapting to create the niche that is best suited to you.

Seedling Niches are big enough to attract many people while also give you some breathing space in order to decide on your permanent niche.

It's a great way to differentiate yourself from the other 500 counsellors in your area, making you more noticeable and attractive to potential clients. While others try to attract everyone and water down their message, you will know who you want to reach and stand out amongst the noise.

Having a niche means you use your marketing to speak directly to potential clients in a way that connects with them. You can use The Empathy Exercise, which we look at in Chapter 15, to get crystal clear on their issues, problems and the solutions they seek and let them know you can help. And as you move forward, you will know what to say on your website, what blogs to write, what to post on social media, how to word leaflets, workshops you might produce etc

However, this is one of the things that often we really push against as counsellors. We think it will restrict the number of clients we attract, restrict the variety of work we have, or we think we aren't 'expert' enough.

I'm going to show you how to give yourself a Seedling niche in order to attract more clients.

With a Seedling Niche, you can focus on one issue or type of client, so you can learn about and understand your ideal clients: what they are currently struggling with (their pain points), and what they want from therapy (their ideal outcome). You'll come to understand what makes them access counselling, their hopes and dreams, their fears and worries. You will be able to attract these clients to you more easily while also helping them in the therapy room via specific training and CPD in the areas that will bring them the greatest benefit.

Also, you'll work with the people and the issues that you're the most passionate about. This makes life so much easier, as when you enjoy something, you become naturally good at it - you just can't help it! You'll read books and articles out of interest rather than because you have to, and you'll be drawn to the subject and become a natural advocate. You'll enjoy your marketing and connecting with and helping people, and creating content (blogs, videos, podcasts) becomes easy for you.

This passion will keep you going through the rough times that will inevitably happen. That extra spark will inspire you to keep going when things are tough, so you can reach the people that need help.

Remember the saying 'Choose a job you love, and you'll never have to work a day in your life'? It's true! One of the benefits of being self-employed is that you can build your practice into whatever YOU want it to be.

Having a niche and getting more training and experience in a specific area means you will become the go-to expert, which will build your professional reputation. Clients will be drawn to you, and the power of word of mouth comes in to force as these people will talk about their positive experiences. Other counsellors will know when you send referrals and feel confident doing so. Over time as you become known, opportunities may appear - to speak on local radio, to be involved in a local event, to collaborate with others on a project.

The aim of this book and everything I do is to show you how to do your marketing as simply and quickly as possible so you can get it done and then go do other things. With the clear focus that a niche brings, you won't waste time trying to attract every client with every issue, saving you confusion and a lot of time.

With all your marketing efforts focussed on one speciality, you will have more success with paid advertisements as they are more highly targeted. It can aid your selection of CPD activities to support your niche. Over time, you will become more highly trained and specialised, and people will pay a premium for a specialist rather than a generalist, so you can increase your prices. Having a niche will benefit you. Being an expert pays!

Having a niche will help clients

Having a speciality means you serve your clients better. You will have a deeper understanding of their needs, it will allow you to attain more specific training targeted to be the most helpful, and you'll amass valuable experience in this field.

All this adds up to a more effective service for your clients, who will get the help they need more efficiently and leave satisfied.

The knock-on effect is that satisfied clients tell other people. They go on to refer you to family and friends leading to word of mouth referrals. This leads to variety in your practice.

When a client has a positive experience of counselling, it benefits the profession as a whole. More positive experiences mean more positive feedback to friends and family, which in turn means more people accessing counselling. It's a win/win situation.

Having a niche makes you more effective as a counsellor, becoming highly trained and experienced in one particular area. This enables you to help clients more effectively and also bring you greater job satisfaction, which is probably why you became a therapist in the first place.

We will take a deeper dive into choosing a niche later in the book, but for now, you're going to choose a Seedling Niche in a broad subject that interests you or you have some experience in.

I suggest you choose from:

Working with loss, which covers bereavement, loss of health, loss of youth, loss of freedom, loss of a job, loss of relationship etc.

Working with anxiety, which covers phobias, panic attacks, OCD, PTSD, stress etc.

Working with self-esteem, which covers people-pleasing behaviour, Childhood emotional neglect and other issues from childhood, feeling worthless, learning to value the self, self-awareness, increasing confidence, assertive communication, bullying etc.

Working with relationships, (individuals) which covers relationships with parents, children, romantic partners, friends, work colleagues etc.

Working with children, whether young children or teenagers.

Working with couples, i.e., two people in the room.

An example of this is if a potential client has experienced miscarriage, they could identify with several of the Seedling Niches I've talked about depending on how they are feeling:

Loss: obviously.

Anxiety: about getting pregnant again, carrying to term, expectations on her from the people around her.

Relationships: How is this affecting her relationships with partner, family and friends?

Self-esteem: How does she feel about herself having had this experience?

Choosing a niche, albeit a temporary one, will help you connect with clients, help clients to connect with you and lets people know when to send referrals to you. When you have decided on a Seedling Niche, you can think about how you'll communicate it.

Imagine this: You're at a party, or the hairdressers and someone says:

'*So, what do you do?*'

You: 'I'm a therapist'

Person '*Oh cool, who do you work with?*'

You: 'Oh, erm...anyone!?'

Person: <*silence*>

Well, it's happened to me - many times! The first question people ask after you say '*I'm a counsellor*' is '*what kind of counsellor*' or '*who do you work with*' which makes me think people expect us to have a speciality. Thinking this through in advance will prevent that awkward '*what do I say here*' moment, followed by kicking yourself for sounding unprofessional or boring. Apart from it being embarrassing, it's also an opportunity lost because every time you speak with someone new is a chance to spread the word about the benefits of counselling and your practice.

You can communicate what you do by using clear, every day, uncomplicated language. Use counselling terms, like 'integrative', humanistic', and 'psychodynamic' is what we call psychobabble, and will not create that connection.

What is psychobabble?

According to Dictionary.com, it's: *'Writing or talk using jargon from psychiatry or psychotherapy without particular accuracy or relevance.'* In practice, this means using words that as therapists will know, but the general public may not know or understand. Words like 'integrative' 'humanistic' 'person-centred' and terms like attachment, Childhood Emotional Neglect (CEN) and even trauma aren't widely understood by the public. For example, often trauma is seen as something that happens following a specific event, like a car accident or a serviceperson returning from a conflict zone. When we use these terms, it creates a disconnect, which is the polar opposite of what we want, which is connection. Remember the Therapy Rebrand mission I talked about in the introduction? We need that connection if we are going to update the image of counselling.

You need a phrase that states very clearly who you are and who you work with. Don't try to complicate it, clear beats clever every time. Here are some ideas:

- I work with young people to reduce anxiety
- I help people get work and life back in balance
- I work with people struggling with loss
- I help people have a better life

See, it can be pretty simple.

In the next chapter, we'll be looking at how to start getting in front of potential clients.

Activity: Your niche statement

In the last chapter, I introduced you to The Pomodoro Technique, where you set a timer and create a time boundary around work. Well, we're going to do that now as you consider how you will introduce yourself using this niche.

Set your timer for 10 minutes and fill in the gaps. Then pick the one you like best.

1. I work with/help [type of person] [do thing] so they can [outcome]. E.g. I work with stressed execs to get a better work/life balance, so they get to see their kids grow up.
2. Counselling/therapy for [client type]
3. [Outcome] for [client type] e.g. Finding peace after bereavement

Practice saying it out loud. Does it sound like you? Will people instantly know what you do? Practice on family and friends – do they instantly know who you work with?

Remember, you're trying to create connection, and clear beats clever every time.

Your Growth Journal: Questions for reflection

- How do you feel about your Seedling Niche?
- How would you feel if this was your full-time niche?

CHAPTER 4 DIRECTORIES

The next thing to do to start attracting clients is to sign up to an online directory. But before we go on, I want to point out that directories have very mixed results and they aren't the right choice for everyone.

There are positives and negatives when it comes to directories:

Positive:

- It gets you in front of people actively looking for a therapist
- It gets you in front of people in your local area
- It's simple to get started

Negative:

- It's not easy to stand out on a directory simply because of the way they are designed. Usually, they have a ticky box list of issues you work with. You're also competing directly with other therapists on things that are often

Directories

- outside of your control, like where you live or work, how you look in a photo etc.
- It's passive, you have no control. Basically, you put up a bio and wait, hoping for the best. You are putting your business in the hands of the gods
- You can be penalised due to your geographic location. For example, I live 6 miles from Lincoln, and because of the number of therapists locally now, I don't show high in results. Sometimes you can pay to appear at the top of results, but after paying a monthly fee and then paying for that on the top, it becomes an expensive way to attract clients
- It can be expensive. There are many directories available now, and some people are on more than one

That said, it's definitely a good thing to try when starting out.

I recommend you invest in an online directory for three to six months and then review to see if it's bringing you results. Sometimes people put their practice on an online directory simply because other people have, but if they aren't bringing you clients, they are just an added expense that could be money better used elsewhere. Ask new clients where they found you, and if it's not a good source of clients for you, then cancel it.

Which one should you choose? That's hard to say, as different countries have different directories, and there are new ones showing up all the time. Which one comes at the top of a Google search for counsellors in your area?

Now let's take a look at setting up your directory entry.

Your photo

You'll need a photo of yourself as people want to know who they are coming to see. You don't have to have professional photos done at this point though you may want to invest in some in the future. Here are a few tips:

- Have a clear, uncluttered background
- Smile! It's been proven that when people see a natural smile, i.e. one where our eyes crinkle, people will be drawn to you
- Use light - natural light is best, but have a few table lights pointing at you if there is no natural light available
- Relax. Potential clients aren't looking for a handsome, pretty or thin therapist so try not to worry about your appearance in that respect. What they want is someone that looks friendly, warm and approachable. As you are about to be photographed, smile and in your head, say '*welcome!*'

What should your entry say?

People aren't interested in you. Sorry to break that to you, but they aren't, at least, not at this stage. All people want to know is '*Can you help me?*'. Your job is to let people know that yes, you can help them.

The fact that you are a therapist means people will assume you are qualified, so telling people all about your qualifications isn't a top priority and wastes valuable space, so do that at the bottom of your entry. Also, make sure there is no psychobabble (check the previous chapter for more on this). Now put yourself in the shoes of potential clients in your Seedling Niche.

- What problems are they struggling with?
- What would be the perfect outcome?

If your Seedling Niche is anxiety, people may struggle with things like sleep, not leaving the house or having a lack of confidence, and the perfect outcome might be to get a good night's sleep, or to go about their day without anxiety putting up barriers, or to feel confident enough to try new things.

Start your directory entry with those. This will let people know that you understand their struggles, and people will start to connect with you. There will be more about creating connection later in the book, but for now, it's more important that you get out there. Done is better than perfect.

Now you need somewhere you can direct people to find more details. It's time to put down some roots.

Activity: Join an online directory

Choose an online directory and put your practice on it. Find out which is bringing in the best results in your area (ask in a therapists Facebook group like my Grow Your Private Practice free Facebook group) see if it has a free trial period and get signed up.

Your Growth Journal: Questions for reflection

- How does it feel to be putting yourself out there?
- What fears are showing up for you? Listen to them and note them down, we'll be covering fears later.

You've just taken a big step forward towards attracting clients. What is a good way for you to celebrate milestones like this? Go and celebrate.

CHAPTER 5 PUTTING DOWN ROOTS

You now have a Seedling Niche and are on an online directory, so it's time to start putting down some roots. This means having somewhere you can direct people to when you don't yet have a website so they can find out a little more about you, and you can start forming connections. I'm going to invite you to use LinkedIn for this.

Why LinkedIn?

LinkedIn is the perfect platform to use to put down roots when starting out, because:

- It's a great place to connect with people locally, so ideal if you work with people on a 1:1 basis
- It's a global platform, so it's also an excellent choice if you work online
- You can use it as a place to publish blogs before you have a website

Putting down roots

- You can start building your social media presence here
- You can direct people to your LinkedIn profile, which can serve as a mini website for you
- You can post videos there
- It's all free!

In the Grow Your Private Practice Club there are several resources about how to use LinkedIn so check out the resources at the end of the book

We shall be looking at social media, blogging, and content creation more closely later in the book, but for now, let's just get started.

Setting up your profile on LinkedIn

As with your directory entry, you'll need a photo on your profile. Many people simply won't engage with profiles that don't have photos, so now isn't the time to be shy. It's a good idea to use the same profile picture on all things online, so use the same picture you used on your directory entry. Remember, people want to see *you*, not a logo.

The bio section on your profile is important, as the first line of your profile is on everything you do on LinkedIn - every post you write and every comment you add. Let's take a look at what you need for a simple, basic profile.

Headline

Your headline - the bit just under your photo and name - should state very clearly who you are and who you help. If you wrote your Niche Statement in chapter 3 you can use that here, so go check that out if you didn't already.

Here are some more ideas:

Putting down roots

- 'Counsellor in [area], helping you to get work and life to balance again'
- 'Helping children have a brighter future'
- 'Helping people move forward after loss'
- 'Working with couples to keep the spark alive'

Limit this to 10-15 words

What not to do

This is prime real estate on LinkedIn where you can get your message out on everything you do so having 'counsellor at [your practice name] counselling' isn't the best use of that space as it's not telling people who you help or what issues you work with. If you need some inspiration, check out what people in other industries are saying but remember, you are unique, so find your own words.

Name

Only have the first name in first name box and surname in the second box. Possibly letters after your name, but nothing more than that. Sneaking in 'counsellor' or psychotherapist' could get you blacklisted.

Amend your URL

When you set up an account on LinkedIn, you will be allocated your own personal URL which will look something like www.linkedin.com/in/1234567. However, having your own LinkedIn URL, which has your name rather than numbers makes you appear professional, and makes sharing easier. For example, mine is https://www.linkedin.com/in/janetravis/ - (come and connect with me!).

LinkedIn URLs are unique, your name might not be available, which means you'll have to be more creative but keep the URL as close to your name as possible. You may need to use a middle initial. No spaces or special characters allowed.

Now you can start filling in your summary.

Summary

The summary is your chance to shine. This is where you can talk about what issues you work with, and who you help. Now that you have a Seedling Niche, you can put yourself in their shoes and consider:

- What problems do they currently have (aka 'pain points')?
- What is the outcome they desire (aka ideal outcome)?

Answering these questions will help you start thinking about the needs of clients, i.e. what brings them to therapy and what they want from it. So, although we are working with a Seedling Niche, this will help you gain greater clarity in all your marketing communications going forward and is a good habit to get into. What we are doing here is kickstarting your private practice, but also this process will kickstart your mind into exploring these new concepts making the process easier later as we start creating something more permanent.

In the summary, let people know you understand their issues and that you can help them. Remember, it's all about them, not you. We're just trying to create a connection, so concentrate on them. Write the summary section focused on 'you' (i.e. the reader), and don't write in the 3rd person. And as discussed in chapter 3, no psychobabble. And read it out loud to check it sounds like you - yes, really!

End with a clear call to action (CTA). What's the ideal next step - to connect with you? To contact you? To read a blog?

EXAMPLE

Life can be amazing, but life can also be challenging, confusing, overwhelming and stressful. And people can be amazing! But also challenging, confusing, overwhelming and stressful. Mostly we can find our own way through life and figure things out ourselves, but sometimes we need a little extra help to make sense of it all. That's where I come in. I'm a [counsellor, psychotherapist] in [area], and I work with people to help take that weight off your shoulders so you can make some sense of it and move forward with your life.

To find out more, email me at jane@myemailaddress, or call me on 01234 567891

Make it as good as you can but don't put yourself under undue pressure, it can be changed and tweaked at any time.

Now work through the other sections, like education etc. LinkedIn will walk you through it.

Activity: Set up your LinkedIn profile

This is a slightly longer activity for you to complete, so I'd suggest breaking it down into Pomodoro chunks:

- Get yourself on LinkedIn - set timer for 15 minutes
- Write your profile - set timer for 20 minutes
- Complete your summary - set timer for 25 minutes

There is potentially a lot to complete, so I'd suggest grabbing your latest CV or job application to collate that information and make your profile a good reflection of you and your practice.

Remember, done is better than perfect. This can be changed and amended at any time, so for now, keep it short and sweet.

How can you attract clients *and* start some new relationships? I'll tell you in the next chapter.

Your Growth Journal: Questions for reflection

- How do I feel now I have put myself on LinkedIn?
- When I read my summary aloud, would I like to work with me? Why?

CHAPTER 6 NETWORKING

If you're a bit of a technophobe, you're going to love this next step because it involves no technology!

You may be interested to know that people trust word of mouth referral far more than any other form of advertising because people trust their friends and family. So as much as I love the online world, nothing will get you remembered more than meeting people in person. We are humans, and connection and communication play a vital part in our lives, and as such, you will be able to connect with people far quicker and be remembered far longer than being seen online.

Business networking can be a phenomenal way to get more referrals to your practice, but as with anything in life, you get out of it what you put in. Go with an open mind and the mindset of getting to know and help people, and you'll not only enjoy it, but you'll also get far better results.

Networking

The things that trip us up here are feeling like we have to:

- Be 'professional', and
- Not cross any personal disclosure boundaries

Both of these things will hamper your ability to connect.

In a business networking event, there is a specific time to talk about your practice, so use that time wisely to spread the word. For the rest of the time, just relax and enjoy the company.

Business networking events are a great way to get known locally. There are many different types at different times of the day, costing different fees and expecting different levels of commitment from you so try a few out to see how you feel about them before you commit to any.

Practically everyone - if not actually everyone, finds business networking a scary prospect, especially when they first get started. It's one of those things you know will be great for your practice, yet just the thought will probably bring you out in hives. This is absolutely normal, and I can't stress this enough.

I can remember my very first networking breakfast meeting many years ago now. I turned up with a churning stomach and sweaty palms. My brain went dead, and I could hardly speak as I was so nervous.

I am a massive introvert (okay, practically a hermit!) so going networking and engaging in small talk isn't somewhere I feel naturally at ease, but I knew it would help my practice. Sometimes we have to 'feel the fear and do it anyway', It's natural to be scared, but it's not ok to let that fear stop you from moving forward and being successful.

Networking

I remember feeling really unsure, not knowing what the 'rules' were and not really sure how it would actually help my business. I tried to portray myself as a Professional Counsellor (capital P, capital C), and I felt a little bit like a 5-year-old pageboy at a wedding that's been made to wear a suit. I thought I had to behave a certain way and talk a certain way, and I've never really pulled off being anything other than me - the person that laughs too loudly has a rude sense of humour and is a bit sweary.

I assumed I had to be very professional and serious because I thought I was selling myself and I wouldn't be taken seriously just being me. (Imposter Syndrome, anyone?)

If I'm being really honest (don't judge me!) I used to see everyone as a potential client, which made me act very differently from how I usually do. I think my desperation for clients must have leaked out of me and been pretty obvious. Although I never directly 'sold' to them (Hi! I'm Jane - are you struggling with anxiety, depression, low mood at the moment? Then here's my card - call me), I'm sure it was written all over my face, and I'm sure this made me appear standoffish, aloof and unnatural.

And what's more, I HATED it!

After persevering and networking for many years, here are some of my top tips:

Form relationships

To get started, this is all you need to be thinking about. Imagine that you are at an event, it might be a breakfast, lunch or evening drinks, and just think about enjoying the event and say to yourself 'I'm here to find out about all these amazing people, what they do, who they work with'. This takes all the pressure off you, and you will be surprised how much easier it will be.

Isolation is a big problem for many therapists and going to networking events is a great way to form business friendships in your local area, friendships that are mutually beneficial.

For me, networking is all about building trusted long-term relationships and taking care of those people around you in your network group. This is what is going to get you results and make your networking so much more fulfilling and worthwhile.

A common misconception is that people think networking is a quick and easy way to attract new clients and they go about the whole thing in a very one dimensional way, almost expecting to leave a meeting with a diary full of new clients. That's simply not the way it works. This is not a short term, quick fix, and you are unlikely to get fast results. Networking is very much a long-term strategy, where mutually beneficial relationships are formed over time, and a whole load of nurturing has been going on. It is then that you will find the people around you will be happy to go out of their way to support you and your business to grow and prosper.

Remember to be yourself, have some fun and develop relationships. Be clear with your message and the results will happen. Over time you will naturally attract the business to you. Once you have built stronger relationships, you will be able to ask for help, introductions and referrals from those around you, as you know that they really care about you and want you to succeed.

Relationships and referrals

It's through the relationships we form the magic happens. When I'm chatting to someone at a networking event that owns a printing business, I get to know, like and trust them. Then when

I'm talking to someone that needs something printing, I will recommend them with confidence. And they will do the same for me. This is where the power lies: through that person, you have access to all their friends and family. You will start getting inquiries from people saying 'such and such told me about you'.

Personal disclosure

For us, as therapists, worries around personal disclosure are never far away, so let me put your mind at rest. After all, just how much are you likely to share about yourself at a networking event? Realistically it simply isn't going to be an issue. They may discover you have a preference for tea over coffee or have a passion for custard creams, but as with any other relationship, you only share what feels comfortable, and you're unlikely to feel comfortable enough to share much of your personal stuff with strangers at a networking event.

I hereby give you permission to relax and enjoy connecting with new people. Just be your usual warm, lovely self, and people will like you, connect with you and remember you.

Concentrate on helping others

This is critical to work on and understand. When you network, it is all about the other person, not you. The key is to stop thinking about what you need and how you feel, it's so much easier to connect with others when you the pressure off yourself and concentrate on them.

Mary Kay Ash says, '*Imagine everyone has an invisible sign around their neck saying, 'make me feel important'*. Be interested, listen, and think about how you can help other people in the room.

You are not there to sell yourself

Don't worry about trying to sell yourself, no one in the room is

Networking

looking to buy. They are looking to form mutually beneficial alliances, so relax. You are connecting with local business people, with the accent on **people**. The people you meet aren't potential clients, they are potential friends, and people respond to this. They also don't respond well to having others view them just as potential clients. Think about it, how do you feel when you know someone wants something from you? I'll tell you how I react - I steer well clear.

Be yourself

When networking, you may think you need to present yourself in a certain way, thinking, 'I'm in a 'professional' environment, so I must present myself as a serious business person who knows their stuff. I must act properly (whatever that means), be ultra professional, and be on my very best behaviour'.

There's nothing wrong with that, and I'm not suggesting that you behave as you do on a night out with your mates, but you need to be yourself and show some personality, and relax so that others can see the person you really are behind that professional exterior. People that are able to be open and friendly are more likely to be remembered. So just be yourself and will accept you for who you are. If you're shy, be shy! Tell people you're a bit shy, just be you. Being shy isn't a crime, and neither is being nervous.

Join a group

Joining a networking group is, in my opinion, far more fulfilling and enjoyable than just attending different ad hoc networking events. For a start, you build relationships with a small group of people, and they become your business friends over time. You will receive a different level of support and develop deeper and

Networking

more meaningful relationships, which are not only more pleasurable but will lead to more business opportunities too.

The thing many people forget about networking is that it's all about having a group of people who really 'get' what you do and what your business is all about. They know, like and trust you wholeheartedly, and they are prepared to proactively recommend and refer you to their contacts. You will then receive referrals from these business friends for years.

Message

The way in which you communicate what you do and how you help your clients is critical for a number of reasons. Your message needs to be memorable, and you need to demonstrate your passion for your practice through expressions, tone and body language. Having a clear and easy to understand description about what you do and who you work with this is what people will remember the most. We look at this in more detail later in the chapter on messaging later in the book.

One final piece of advice on this subject. Be sure you don't use jargon and keep your language simple, so people will understand what your business is all about - no psychobabble. Networking is all about forming connections, and psychobabble creates a disconnect.

Elevator pitch

Many (but not all) business networking events include a 60-second pitch, where you talk about your business to the people on your table for 60 seconds. And it's literally 60 seconds, it's timed, and when your time is up, you have to stop talking. This is the part where you can knock yourself out and tell people

Networking

whatever it is you want to tell them about your practice, which could be:

- Who you work with
- What issues you address
- How clients may feel after therapy
- Why you're passionate about your niche

Or you can give them a couple of tips on some common issues, like getting a good night's sleep or improving your work-life balance.

It's important to practice your elevator pitch in advance as this means you can plan what to say and feel more confident when you say it. Write down your elevator pitch and time yourself saying it, so it's exactly 60 seconds long. Read it out loud several times, and when you have the timing right, write bullet points on a card as an aide memoir.

You will probably feel nervous before you talk, but that's perfectly normal. I've never, ever done an elevator pitch without feeling nervous. I've also never done a perfect pitch, and usually manage to trip over some words, my mind goes blank, or I get my timing wrong. In my experience, very few people feel comfortable doing them so are very forgiving of mistakes.

Networking is one of the few times we as therapists need business cards, so have some very simple ones made up to include your name, email, phone number and LinkedIn URL. These are only temporary so don't overthink them, you can always get some new ones after you get a website and get clearer on branding at some point in the future.

After the event, you'll have a collection of business cards you will have received from others. Send them a connection request

Networking

with a short message on LinkedIn saying that it was lovely meeting them at the event and add a short, personalised note and that you'd like to connect with them.

Engagement

When you go networking, it's important to be totally in the present and 100% engaged with whom you're talking to at that given moment in time. Listening is something you are naturally good at, so give the person you are speaking with your undivided attention. Try asking some questions to find out about that person and their business. Things like:

- Have you been in business long?
- What do you like most about being a [job title]?
- Who do you mainly work with?
- Where are you based?
- Are you a regular at this event?

To be an effective networker, you will need to be prepared to take action. This doesn't mean you just turn up for the regular meetings that your group organises, it means arranging 1:1's with other members (going for a coffee to get to know each other and each other's businesses better), and doing helpful things for others like refer people to them. Taking action is simply another element of networking, and if you do this well, you will be able to truly enjoy the benefits of networking at its very best.

Keep it upbeat

A lot of what we do is working with pretty serious stuff: grief, abuse, loss, depression, etc., and many people will feel awkward talking about these things. When talking about what you do avoid the 'before' part of the equation, i.e. working with depression, loss etc. and talk about the 'after', the bit where people report feeling more confident, have better communication, better relationships, etc. I talk about this in the 'features Vs benefits' section of the messaging chapter 14.

Activity: Networking search

Do a search for 'networking [your area]' and choose a meeting to attend. Take action and start making some connections.

Your Growth Journal: Questions for reflection

- When I think about networking, what am I afraid of and why?
- Write about a time when you felt anxious about something new, but when you did it, you enjoyed it. How can you apply that learning to networking?

Kickstart conclusion

Well, that wasn't too bad, was it! You can now relax, as you have all the main bases covered: somewhere to direct people to for more information on you, a social media platform, somewhere to blog and a place to connect with local people. In fact, you can keep marketing your practice in this way for as long as you like. It's a great way to get started and earn more before you start thinking about investing in a website. All this for very little financial investment. Not too shabby, eh?

I wonder what's been coming up for you as you've been working through this quickstart chapter? Worries about being visible, procrastination and perfectionism holding you back? Maybe you don't feel good enough? Perhaps you have a touch of anxiety? Well look, that's okay. In fact, that's totally normal, and in the next section, we'll be looking at how to grow your private practice despite these worries.

PART 2: MINDSET

CHAPTER 7 IMPOSTER SYNDROME

Do you know Maya Angelou? She published seven autobiographies, three books of essays, several books of poetry, and is credited with a list of plays, movies, and television shows spanning over 50 years. She received dozens of awards and more than 50 honorary degrees.

She once said:

"I have written 11 books, but each time I think 'Uh-oh, they're going to find out now. I've run a game on everybody, and they're going to find me out.'

Yes, Maya Angelou gets Imposter Syndrome.

Picture this: Me sitting in front of a Google Doc, the flashing cursor mocking me. I want to write a blog, but I can't think because of my inner critic shouting at me.

'Why would people be interested in anything you say?'

'You don't even know about this stuff; you're just winging it.'

'If you write this, you'll be uncovered as a fraud.'

Welcome back Imposter Syndrome I knew you'd show up!

And yes, as I write this book, Imposter Syndrome is always with me, sometimes whispering in my ear, sometimes shouting, always bullying. So, what is Imposter Syndrome, how does it affect us, and how can we manage it?

What is Imposter Syndrome?

Imposter Syndrome is a term first coined by Dr. Pauline R. Clance and Dr. Suzanne A. Imes in 1978 and means you don't internalise your own accomplishments despite evidence to the contrary. It's the feeling of having faked your way to where you are now and that somehow someday you'll be unmasked as the fraud that you are. It's a feeling of being out of your depth.

It's when you want to:

- Write a blog, but stop yourself because you don't feel you have anything worthwhile to say
- Deliver a workshop but don't feel you have enough knowledge
- Start in private practice, but think people wouldn't come to you

It's a very common thing. It's said to affect 70% of people at some point, but personally, I think this figure is way higher, especially among women. It doesn't discriminate, it's happy to bully celebrities, sportspeople, businesspeople, politicians (though possibly not Mr Trump…) no matter how successful they are.

Imposter Syndrome is common in the counselling profession

Imposter Syndrome is common in counsellors and therapists because it's our job to help clients with these sorts of insecurities. Therefore we tell ourselves we *should* know what to do, and we *should* feel differently, which goes to prove we clearly know nothing, we're just rampant frauds and will soon be found out, publicly shamed and humiliated... Which only adds to the problem, as we feel more pressure to be all knowledgeable and yet less able to talk about it with others.

I have a saying that we are human first, counsellor second. We have exactly the same feelings, worries and issues as everyone else. Being a counsellor doesn't mean we miraculously know the answer to all of life's questions so take that pressure off yourself. If you're struggling with something, get some help. Just because you're a therapist, it doesn't mean you have to have your life all figured out. You're a work in progress, just like everyone else. You will have exactly the same feelings, worries and issues as everyone else and being a therapist doesn't change that.

Imposter Syndrome has absolutely no relation to your actual skills, qualities or abilities. In fact, the higher up you go the more likely this feeling will be spooking around in your head. Although it is called a syndrome, it isn't a mental health issue or anything that is wrong with you, it's simply part of the human condition. We all have it, to a greater or lesser extent. We have it now, our ancestors had it, and our future selves will have it.

However, it can't be ignored because it will tell you that you have no right to be here, to be a therapist, to try and help other people and expect to be paid for it. If left to its own devices, it

Imposter Syndrome

will tell you that you don't belong and constantly poke at all of your insecurities. Imposter Syndrome is a problem because it can:

- Stop you from moving forward and improving
- Make you take another qualification rather than taking clients
- Hamper your success because you don't do the things that will move your practice forward
- Stop you helping the people that need it because they simply don't know you are there

Where does Imposter Syndrome come from?

Probably childhood, because as we know only too well, most things come from childhood experiences. It seems to come from the fact that we know ourselves and we know our thoughts, actions and feelings. You know about the time you stole sweets from Woolworths or smiled inwardly when someone you're jealous of fell flat on their face. You know about the times you didn't tip, or didn't let someone out at a junction, or snapped at a salesperson. You know about your secret sexual fantasies and all manner of other personal things you might partake in the privacy of your bedroom and bathroom.

We know ourselves from the inside, every shameful, unkind, freaky thought, but we don't see that part of other people. We only see what they show us, and what they show us is the Instagram version of their lives, all fun, smiles, friends, and travel. We see the healthy green smoothie, not the family-sized chocolate bar washed down by wine.

Imposter Syndrome

We only know a few people well enough to see underneath that, and even then, we don't see what's in the murkier bits and we never will. Thankfully!

It's hard to believe that other people have just as many secret thoughts and distasteful habits as we do because we simply never get to see it.

I've always loved the Wheatus song 'Teenage Dirtbag', where the character is in love with a girl, and laments:

'But she doesn't know who I am,

And she doesn't give a damn about me

'Cause I'm just a teenage dirtbag, baby'

He knows all about his teenage angst, his 'learning about his body' sessions, his weirdness, his feelings of being 'different'. And (spoiler alert!) they get together because she's a teenage dirtbag too. I love a happy ending.

We all live our lives knowing all about the weird freaky stuff that runs through our heads, but we don't see that in other people. They (other people) put their best foot forward, hide their secrets, and we take them at face value. In turn, we put our best foot forward and hide our secrets, but we know it's just an act because we know the terrible truth.

But we ALL feel that way, every one of us, and we live with it. Then sometimes it rises and slaps us round the face as Imposter Syndrome, with things like:

- I don't deserve this
- I shouldn't be here
- I was just lucky
- It was a fluke

- I'm not good enough
- I'll be uncovered as a fraud

We are only too aware of our own human failings and assume others have their lives together, despite knowing logically, that's not really the case.

How it affects you?

Imposter Syndrome is serious and can have a detrimental effect on your practice. It causes self-sabotage like procrastination and perfectionism (which we'll be looking at later) as a way to prevent your true self being uncovered. It stops you moving forward personally and stops your business success because you don't do the things that will bring growth.

Most importantly, it stops you helping people that need it. There are people that need your help and would be your perfect client, but if they don't know you're there, they may never even access that help.

Ask yourself:

- How many people want to open a private practice, but carry on volunteering?
- Or want to write a book, but tell themselves they can't?
- How many people want to live stream, but are crippled by fear?
- How many want to write a blog?
- Or deliver workshops?
- Or approach businesses to offer services?
- Or go networking?

What to do if you suffer from Imposter Syndrome

Thankfully, there are lots of things you can do to help yourself.

Acknowledge your feelings

The first thing you can do is actually acknowledge your feelings of incompetence and remind yourself that everybody feels this way sometimes and that it's simply a part of the human condition. You can't do anything unless you first acknowledge it and see it for what it is.

You may want to hide and keep these terrible truths to yourself, but that will just exacerbate things so talking to people really is important. Not only will they be able to reassure you that they sometimes feel this way too but also remind you of your qualities, traits and accomplishments.

Insecurities like this swirling around in your head just get more and more momentum, like a hurricane getting bigger and more powerful. Talking to someone can help take the power out of it, like when the hurricane touches land. Tell someone, whether a friend, family member, your supervisor or in the Grow Your Private Practice Facebook group, where you'll get plenty of support.

For me, when I'm on top of my game, it's not an issue, but if I'm feeling unsure, lacking confidence or trying something new, it can really stop me in my tracks.

I can remember a time when Imposter Syndrome ambushed me and slapped me hard to the point that I had a whole weekend of having to deal with excruciating feelings of unworthiness.

Imposter Syndrome

Instead of trying to ignore it, I used that time to really explore what was happening for me.

I have a tendency to keep things to myself, so in a Facebook group I felt safe in, I opened up - very tentatively to start with - about my feelings and gave a vague description of currently struggling with Imposter Syndrome. The responses I got were amazing. I didn't get 'aaw hun, but you're great' throwaway answers, nor did I get comments that made me feel silly. No, what I got were responses from women that I admire empathising with me and sharing that they often feel very similar. This felt amazing.

I spent the whole weekend on a mission of self-care, which took the form of cleaning and tidying my house to make my living space more comfortable. All the time, I binge listened to podcasts and books on Audible to help me with what I was currently working through. I also took to my journal and did some stream-of-consciousness writing.

By the end of the weekend, I felt so much better. Not only did I have a comfortable, tidy and clean house, I felt supported by other people, and I felt cared for by myself.

What revealed itself to me is my process for getting through these times. I now know my process is:

- Decide to do something new
- Have a major wobble and think the world is going to come crashing down around my ears
- Talk myself off the edge
- Do the thing
- Carry on living my life till the next time

Imposter Syndrome

When I start hearing that familiar 'who are you to think you can do this?' negative self-talk, I now understand what it is and that it will pass so I don't beat myself up about it. I recognise it for what it is - Imposter Syndrome, and my panic is just me being me going through my process. This helps me put it into perspective. It's not real, it's my insecurities, and this provides comfort that the massive wobble is temporary. If I ride out the storm, things will feel better again.

I've found my way to handle Imposter Syndrome, and if you allow yourself to accept and sit with it, you will too. I wonder if you already know your process?

Mindfulness

Another thing you can do to help with this is to practice mindfulness. Use it to notice feelings and also raise awareness of any feelings of inadequacy. Notice:

- When do these feelings arise?
- What are you doing?
- Where do they show up in the body?

Does it come from fight, flight or freeze? For me, I tend to want to run away and hide, or I become paralysed by fear, but maybe you get flustered, frustrated and angry. Maybe physically you feel your heart racing, feel sick or lightheaded.

Notice what's happening to your thoughts - is your head full of chatter and you can't concentrate? Maybe you struggle to remember things, maybe anxiety makes you feel locked inside your own head and unable to focus on things going on around you.

Find your inner cheerleader

There's a popular story of the grandfather that takes his grandson out into the forest. He tells his grandson there are two wolves fighting within us - a bad wolf that is full of hatred, anger, darkness and shame, and a good wolf full of hope, kindness, compassion and honesty. The boy asks which is the one that wins, and the wise grandfather says 'the one that you feed'.

When Imposter Syndrome hits, your inner critic is handed a megaphone in order to let you know just how incapable you are. Ouch!

It's time to rally the troops, because for every yin there is yang, for light there is dark, and within you, you have both an inner critic and the angelic version, your inner cheerleader. Your inner cheerleader is always there to spur you on, always ready to support you and give you a mental high five.

Identify that the inner critic is only one part of your mind, and you could choose not to listen to them and listen to the inner cheerleader instead.

Feed the good wolf and fight the bad wolf.

Repeat some positive affirmations.

The brain is an exquisite piece of design, but the brain can be easily fooled. It doesn't know the truth, it simply believes whatever it's told, so if you tell it you are useless, it will believe you. Start telling it how wonderful you are instead.

Saying the right words to yourself works even if you don't quite believe it yet. Put simply, positive affirmations are positive phrases or statements used to challenge negative or unhelpful thoughts.

Practising positive affirmations is extremely simple, and all you need to do is pick a phrase and repeat it to yourself. Try:

- I recognise that my negative thoughts are irrational, and now I'm going to stop these fears
- I am not afraid to keep going, and I believe in myself
- I have come this far, and I am proud of myself
- I release negative feelings and thoughts about myself
- I believe in who I am
- I am on a journey, ever-growing and developing
- I believe in myself, and trust my own wisdom
- I am a successful person
- I am confident and capable of what I do

Repeating these affirmations will make the voice of your inner cheerleader stronger. Write down some positive affirmations that resonate with you (you can search affirmations on Google), say them out loud and say them internally. Repeat often, as many times a day as you can manage. Make one your screensaver, doodle it on your journal or print it out and keep it by you.

Best friend

Imagine your best friend said to you 'I've just qualified as a therapist, but I think it was a mistake - I just got lucky, and now I'm expected to know how to help people. I can't do it'.

What would you say? Probably something like 'I know how hard you've worked; I know how passionate you are about this and the commitment you have for this cause. We all feel insecure sometimes, but you can totally do this because it's what you were born to do'.

Imposter Syndrome

The next time you hear those doubts creep in, talk to yourself like you would your best friend. I bet you'd never say such harsh things to anyone else.

Drop the comparisons

It's hard not to compare yourself with other people, but comparisons will drive you crazy. The biggest issue I have with comparisons is we simply don't know the facts. What people present to the world isn't always a fair representation of who they really are.

I remember reading a blog that had an image of a young couple on holiday, in love and smiling, beautiful. The author was the woman in the picture, who explained that just before that photo was taken, they were arguing, and they broke up soon after returning home. I bet you've done it yourself, been to a party and had a miserable time but smiled for the camera.

The other person you're comparing yourself against may be good at hiding their insecurities - or they may just be really good at what they do. Good for them! It takes absolutely nothing from you because you have your own skillset your own knowledge, experience, thoughts and ideas. It's like comparing apples and oranges. No one has to be better, just different. We'll look at this more in Chapter 8, overcome self-sabotage.

Start a smile file

I've already talked about the benefits of having a journal/progress log where you can record all your achievements, no matter how small. Every compliment, every comment, every time you help a client, every time you help someone in a Facebook group. Record it all, so if Imposter Syndrome hits you have documented evidence to prove you're pretty fabulous, actually.

Journal

I'm sure I don't have to tell you about the benefits of journaling and its ability to help us sort through our feelings, so write about how you're feeling, write about your worries and your fears and then reflect on them. You will be amazed at the number of aha's you get.

For example, if you had critical parents, maybe you always expect a harsh response. Did they expect 100% from you so now anything less than perfect doesn't hit the mark? Remember, perfectionism isn't about wanting to be perfect, it's a fear we're never quite good enough.

You can be creative in the way you journal. For example, some people draw instead of writing. The important thing is discovering and reflecting on feelings.

Examining these feelings helps you find the origin of your story. Your journal will show you where these feelings originally came from and dealing with these types of things will help put Imposter Syndrome to bed.

Accept that you had some part in the success you've had

It's easy to dismiss or discount our successes and label them as luck or coincidence, but is that really true? Even if you were just in the right place at the right time, you were still there! You will have had to work for your accomplishments. For example, in your counselling training, you worked for and achieved your qualifications by:

- Attending lessons
- Completing assignments
- Completing journals
- Seeing clients in placement

Imposter Syndrome

- Possibly sitting an exam

That takes work, it doesn't happen by accident. You worked for your qualifications and got them because of that work. You deserve them.

Separate feelings from fact, because you may *think* you're a fraud, but that doesn't mean you are.

Don't rush into getting another qualification

You may be tempted to get more qualifications. For example, you get a client with anxiety, so you take a course about anxiety, and you get a client that's suffered from bereavement, so you get training on bereavement etc. Not necessarily a bad thing, but remember clients want to be heard, for you to be there, and to connect. The quality of the counsellor/client relationship is so important, don't underestimate its power.

If taking another qualification is part of your future plans and is to do with your niche then go ahead, but if you enrol in courses in a 'reactive' way, i.e. reacting to a new client's needs, this may be a form of Imposter Syndrome.

Having a string of qualifications means you're a good learner, it doesn't necessarily mean you are a good counsellor. Trust yourself. Trust the process. You are good enough.

Give yourself permission to not have to know everything

You don't need to always know the answer, so take the pressure off. Occasionally getting things wrong doesn't mean you don't know what you're doing or are a fake.

I love what Denise Duffield Thomas says in *'Don't be a guru - be a contributor instead.'*

'As soon as I gave myself permission to contribute to the conversation (of women and money), and not have to be a guru or expert, then my business became fun. If you really care about a topic, be a contributor. Who cares if you don't know everything? You don't have to be the best to make a difference to someone.'

Accept that you're going to get things wrong

We all get things wrong. Basically, you just can't grow without making mistakes. We'll be looking at this closer in the next chapter.

So, publishing a blog that's not 'The Perfect Blog' is not only ok, it's necessary. How else can you learn?

Failure is fun! Think of it that way - if you're failing, you're taking action. You're real. You can't be fake and fail at the same time. Failure will eventually lead to victory. In fact, failure is the only way to get to victory, and it's the only way to enjoy it because you can only enjoy something once you've tasted the opposite.

Do things before you're ready

If we waited until we were ready for kids, we'd have a dwindling population. But usually we have the baby, *then* figure out what to do with it! It's the same with business. If you wait until you have all your ducks in a row, you'll never start, because there is always more to do. It's a magical, never-ending to-do list.

Acting before you are ready is like penicillin for Impostor Syndrome. It helps you build up immunity and the more you act before you're ready, the more you'll realise that you're never really ready for anything. But neither is anyone else.

This is why I tend to say yes to things, and then work out how to do it later. For example, I was asked to talk at a BACP conference. I'd never done one before and was pretty terrified, but I said yes and worked out what to do afterwards.

When you look around you at the success other people have, I'd like you to gently remind yourself that they are just normal people and that they have their secrets and fears and weirdness too. As therapists, we are in the privileged position of getting to hear the deep dark fears of our clients, so you'll know that the fears we have are pretty universal. I've had beautiful people tell me they are ugly, intelligent people tell me they are stupid, kind people tell me they are horrible, people exhausted from giving to others tell me they are selfish. What we think is often simply not true. Don't believe everything you think. We're all teenage dirtbags in the end because we are all merely human.

Reward yourself

Business is hard. Life is hard. You're doing your best, so reward yourself often. Pause when you finish something and allow yourself time to celebrate. Take in the feeling of accomplishment and let it wash over you. Allow yourself to fully appreciate that despite your fears, you did it. The definition of being brave is being scared but doing it anyway. You have shown bravery, now acknowledge that.

Just because we are therapists and know how to help other people with insecurities, it doesn't mean we don't have our own, and just because we have insecurities, it doesn't mean we can't be extremely effective as counsellors and help many others. Just because Imposter Syndrome is shouting at you doesn't mean you've nothing valuable to say or can't offer your thoughts and opinions.

You are qualified, you are passionate, and you can help people. But you can't help them if they don't know you're there.

Recognise Imposter Syndrome for what it is - a nasty little bully that's lying to you. We have to stand up to bullies. Don't let the bully win.

In the next chapter, we'll take a closer look at mindset issues and sneaky self-sabotage that will hold you back.

Activity: My personal statement exercise

Grab some paper and a pen, and set a timer for 20 minutes: We're going to uncover why you're totally good enough to be a counsellor!

List ALL the things you've achieved in your life, like:

- Your swimming badges
- Cycling proficiency
- Brownie/Cub badges
- Awards
- Flick through your whole life and add anything you can remember. Work right up to now, so your school qualifications, that you had a part in the school play used to help your brother to learn to read, you volunteered to work Christmas Eve so your colleague could be with their kids, that your client thanked you for helping them
- Now, list all the things you are good at. Things like 'I am always on time', or 'I make amazing chilli'
- Now, write your personal statement in 'I' statements:

I am _____: I am good at attention to detail, at listening, I am compassionate etc.

And that little voice that's telling you it was nothing special? Well, be aware of it, see how often it crops up, and say to it 'thank you for your input, but you're wrong'.

Keep your personal statement close, and keep on adding any and all positive achievements, big and small. The qualification you just got, the compliment, the hug from a friend. This is you.

Your Growth Journal: Questions for reflection

- How does Imposter Syndrome show up for you, and how can you protect yourself from it?
- How is the public you different from the private you?

CHAPTER 8 OVERCOME SELF SABOTAGE

Here's the thing. Marketing is actually pretty straightforward if you let it be. You decide who you want to work with and use one of the methods I talk about in this book to connect with those people. What isn't so easy is managing your mindset and sidestepping the self-sabotaging that you will inevitably do.

- Anxiety whispers 'what if's...' in your ear
- Comparisons whisper 'everyone is doing so much better than you.'
- Imposter Syndrome whispers 'you'll be uncovered as a fraud.'
- Shiny Object Syndrome whispers 'don't do that, do this instead.'
- Perfectionism whispers that 'it's not good enough.'
- And they all beckon procrastination along to stop you from achieving anything

Why? Because we're all human, that's why! But you don't have to have everything all worked out to enable you to work with clients successfully. You don't have to have the perfect life with perfect relationships, be the perfect parent, or the perfect son/daughter. It's ok to just be normal, to argue with your partner, shout at your kids, swear at other drivers and like a good old gossip with friends. That doesn't make you either a bad therapist or a bad person, it makes you real and authentic. The people in your life want you to be you, with all your quirks and idiosyncrasies. It's what makes you the fabulous, unique individual that you are.

As a therapist, you don't have to know all the answers, you just need the right questions to enable people to find their own answers. You are a work in progress, and if you live to be 100 (and I hope you do), you will still be learning about yourself, others, relationships and life every day. There never becomes a point where, like Neo in 'The Matrix', you say 'I know life'.

As a human, you will have highs and lows, insecurities and self-sabotages, worries and fears - it's how you are made and is all perfectly normal. As a private practitioner, part of the work you need to do to grow your practice is personal development. Working on your mindset to protect yourself from your self-sabotage to grow both personally and professionally. Before we take a look at some of the practical things to do about attracting clients, let's take a look at some of the things that might trip you up before you even start.

Fear

When you think about running a private practice, about attracting clients, being visible, getting your name out there and telling people what you do, what happens for you?

Perhaps you feel excited at the prospect. But perhaps you feel some anxiety too. It could be just a small tinge of anxiety, or it could be a full-on panting, sweating, tummy-turning major panic attack!

That's ok!

Not only is it ok to feel anxious, but it's also absolutely normal. This is true for all business owners in all industries, not just therapists. It's completely normal to feel anxious when doing something new - we're wired for it! You know this. You probably work with this all the time.

Anxiety means nothing more than you're doing something that's nudging you out of your comfort zone. It doesn't mean you can't do it, it's not right for you or you are destined for failure. It just means YOU ARE NORMAL!! (Whatever that is.)

Anxiety is fine. Listen to it, explore it and work with it.

If you feel like an imposter? That's great - you can work on that!

Maybe you worry people will criticise? That's great, you can work on that too!

You worry people won't be interested in what you have to say? That's brilliant because you can totally work on these things.

Feeling anxious and allowing yourself to explore your anxiety means you can uncover really important stuff to work on, work through, learn about yourself and ultimately protect yourself from in the future. Anxiety is only a problem when we run away from it and hide, because hiding won't move you forward, either in business or life.

- Hiding won't attract clients

- Hiding means you can't do the thing you love and are passionate about
- Hiding doesn't bring success
- Hiding doesn't bring money

Hiding only perpetuates the 'I can't do this' feeling and will keep holding you back throughout your life

I know this first-hand. My niche is relationships with food. It's something I am extremely passionate about, knowledgeable in and feel excited about making a difference in the lives of people trapped in destructive eating patterns. So far, so good. But then fear kicked in. I am not a thin person, which has previously brought me criticism and ridicule from my family. I started imagining what people would think of me or say behind my back. Things like 'why does she think she can help others when she clearly can't help herself', or people laughing at me. I'd worry about nasty comments online making fun of me. I'd worry that no one would take what I was saying seriously, and I'd become the butt of jokes.

These fears crippled me to the point that I almost changed my niche to something that made me feel less vulnerable. But I didn't, because I knew helping people with issues around eating, food, body image and self-esteem was something I cared about deeply, and it was something I could change lives with. If I was going to work with the people, I felt most passionate about helping, I'd have to find a way forward. How many people wouldn't have been helped if I'd listened to those fears? How many people would still be trapped their binge/starve life, constantly dieting, purging, hating themselves and feeling worthless?

Overcome Self Sabotage

Stepping out of your comfort zone will bring up fears and anxieties, and you'll have to revisit them many times, so how you handle it is important. Approach them with curiosity, 'that's interesting, I wonder why I feel...?' And be gentle with yourself, you can't bully your fears away.

The fears and anxieties we have about being in private practice can sometimes be surprising and uncover some important and interesting new information that will help you understand yourself better.

Reframe

Here's a really simple way to reframe this. Every time you notice anxious thoughts creeping into your head and you say to yourself I can't do this, I'm going to fail, I'm nervous, change what you say to 'I feel excited about this'. Simple, but it works! There have been many of studies about this, and time and again it's been proven to be highly effective. Even better - it doesn't matter if you don't believe it, you can still trick your brain into believing it.

This is because the physical response to anxiety is the same as the physical response to excitement - your heart beats faster, your tummy flips you have tingly fingers. It works - give it a go!

Fear of failure

> *"Failure is not the opposite of success; it's part of success."* Arianna Huffington

A common fear when starting in private practice is 'What if I can't make this work?' This fear is sometimes enough to stop you in your tracks and not even get started in your private practice. It'll make you procrastinate until you get the perfect website (hint - there is no such thing!) or even go and get more qualifications,

Overcome Self Sabotage

which is a form of procrastination. But here's the thing: the most important thing in private practice, the thing that will attract clients and bring you the success that you desire isn't having more and more qualifications. It's about working on your fears in order to be visible, connect with people and let them know who you are and how you can help.

Failure is good!

In business as in life, we learn from failure. We learn some of our biggest and most important lessons from the biggest failures that we have.

If you decide to invest in some leaflets to deliver in your local area and the phone doesn't ring, then you have some important information there. What did you do? What didn't you do? Where did you put your leaflets? What did you put on your leaflets? Was there too much information? Too little? Could they have been clearer? Could the design be improved? Were they speaking to your ideal clients? Did they have a clear 'Call To Action' (CTA)?

The fact that you printed leaflets and got out there in the community is a massive win and should be celebrated no matter what the outcome. You left your comfort zone, and you did it. You are one large step ahead of someone who has never done that, so congratulate yourself.

Record all your progress, and I mean everything, no matter how small, because so much progress comes from those tiny baby steps, but they aren't always noticed in the same way as children grow. If you have a child, you don't notice how much it's growing every day, but when you run into someone you've not seen for ages, and they say, ' oh wow haven't they grown!' you realise that your baby is growing up! Keep a record, and then you'll be able to look back and see just how far you've come, and how much progress you've made. The next time you do a leaflet drop, you can use that experience to have a better idea of how to do it and a far greater chance of it being successful.

Failure is good, it means you are learning.

Fear of success

What if I fail is a common and obvious fear, but something equally common but a lot less obvious is a fear of success. This is to do with the negative consequences that may happen if you are successful in your venture. Some examples may be:

- What if I experience jealousy from others - my peers, family, friends, partner?
- What if I find it too hard?
- What if I get overwhelmed?
- What if I get burnt out?
- What if I'm not good enough?
- What if I can't help my clients?
- What if people think I have ideas above my station?

Fear of success is confusing. After all, we all want to succeed, don't we? On a head level, yes, but sometimes on a deeper heart level, we have fears to overcome. This is something you might experience in the therapy room with clients.

My niche, as I said, is relationships with food which means I often see people who want to lose weight and are constantly dieting but can't seem to make any progress and are often actually putting weight on. They have a fantasy that losing weight magically takes away all their problems and fears, and they will become confident, sexy, do all the things they want to do that the weight stopped them from doing. They will travel, dance, dress differently and be more successful.

Then they start to lose weight, get to a certain size and hit a plateau.

What actually happens as they get closer to 'success' is they come face-to-face with their fears. Maybe being slimmer means they will attract more attention from the opposite (or same) sex, which is scary because this could mean getting hurt. Maybe being slimmer will attract more sexual attention from their partner, and they no longer fancy them and being overweight may have been the excuse they've used to avoid physical intimacy.

Maybe being slimmer will attract more attention and mean you have to address the fact your current relationship is not making you happy, and a decision needs to be made. Maybe you think being slimmer means having to act differently, to be more of an extrovert, to dress flirtier or be sexier. Being overweight is the excuse you need to not do things you don't want to do. Things like 'oh I can't go swimming I don't want people to see me in a swimming costume', and you never do.

In 'The Big Leap', Gay Hendricks calls it an upper limit problem. We reach a level where we feel comfortable and don't think we deserve more or better, so we sabotage ourselves instead.

I experienced this when starting the Grow Your Private Practice Club. I was so excited, the possibilities of where I could take it were amazing, but I had a real worry that was difficult to explain to people.

I remember having coffee with a friend and telling them I was feeling anxious but couldn't really put my finger on why. She thought I was worried about it failing and try to offer me reassurance and support. But I wasn't worried it would fail, what I was really worried about was that it would be successful and that I would be so busy that it would take up all of my time, and people would want too much from me which would leave me feeling spent and exhausted. Interesting, right?

It comes from a couple of different places. My background, obviously. I was always there for other people, I was a people pleaser, a rescuer, my place in life was to help others.

I used to run a blog called Self Care for People Pleasers, which was very successful and which I enjoyed enormously. However, I closed it down because I would get several emails a day from people struggling, suffering and wanting my help. I'd receive a long email about the pain and cruelty in their life, and I couldn't just ignore it, so I would always reply even if it was a short email suggesting places and ways to get help.

I felt overwhelmed and helpless that I couldn't help them more. Alongside this, I also felt angry that these horrendous stories were showing up in my inbox several times every day and then felt guilty that I felt angry. It was a real vicious circle. It felt too much for me, so I closed that business down. If I'd had better boundaries, who knows how successful that would have been?

This was important intel as it meant I was able to explore this more fully and put boundaries in place to help protect myself from feeling overwhelmed.

I also realised how I have a tendency to feel overwhelmed and then walk away. I walked away from Friends With Food (another online business where I let my fears about my own size stop me from moving a business forward) Just as I also walked away from Self-care For People Pleasers.

I didn't want this to happen again. I knew there was a way for me to be successful AND manage my feelings. This realisation was so important for my business and myself because I worked out what I was really worried about - being overwhelmed by people's needs, so was able to explore this a little deeper and protect myself by setting boundaries.

The answer to the fear of success is boundaries - time boundaries, practising good self-care, only seeing clients when it's suitable for you, and only working within your capabilities. If you're feeling the fear:

- Stop
- Breathe
- Sit with the feeling
- Journal
- Get help
- Learn from it

Keep moving forward. Baby steps are absolutely fine, you're still making progress.

Perfectionism

On the face of it, perfectionism can seem like a good thing - attention to detail and having high standards are good, right? Well, not necessarily. Perfectionism can stop you from actually achieving anything. For example, you write a blog, but it takes forever as you:

- Look for the perfect subject
- Perfect every sentence
- Perfect layout
- Find the perfect title

- The perfect image
- Perfect the SEO
- Perfect CTA (Call To Action)
- Perfect social media posts

Can you see how this isn't useful in business and stops you moving forward, attracting clients, being successful and making money? Perfectionism will hold you back.

Action is the antidote to fear because action creates progress and growth. Stop thinking and planning, researching and preparing to blog, it's time to just crack on and start writing! Start before you're ready, get stuck in and remember, if you see a typo, or want to add or take away from what you have written, you can.

You could wait until this time next year to get started while you research, plan and learn, or you can start before you're ready, now, today and in a year's time have a huge amount of valuable experience and a blog that's attracting clients.

Procrastination

Well, what can I say about procrastination! I remember one year when I had less than a week to complete my tax return, I decided that I needed to sort out my sock drawer. I'm sure most of my housework only gets done because I'm procrastinating doing something else! Procrastination is avoidance. What about these?

- You spend hours 'researching' a blog, but don't write a word
- You spend hours making small tweaks to your website but don't do anything productive

- You spend hours designing your swanky new business cards which will only ever gather dust in a drawer somewhere

The struggle is real! I feel it every day. But if you want to have a successful practice, attract clients and make money, you have to keep on top of it.

A great way to manage perfectionism and procrastination is to put time boundaries around tasks. Using The Pomodoro Technique works like a dream - I introduced you to it in chapter 2.

Comparisons

We talked about this in the last chapter, but here we're looking at making business comparisons.

Do you ever compare yourself to other therapists? We all do it to an extent, and it's tough. I hear it all the time in the therapy room, and I bet you do too. Things like 'other people don't feel like this', or 'why can't I just let this go like other people', or 'when other people have things happen, they don't go to pieces.

I say, how do you know? You've no idea what's going on in their lives, you've no idea how they arrive in their current situation. It's exactly the same for us as therapists. We see other counsellors who appear more successful, get more clients, more quickly, and it can feel like a slap in the face when you're struggling to get your practice established.

On a head level, you know you shouldn't compare. But on a heart level, you're screaming *'why not me - what's wrong with me?!?'*

Stop that. There is nothing wrong with you!

The problem is, we don't use a level playing field, we don't compare like for like. And there's a reason for this - we have absolutely no idea about the circumstances of the other person we are comparing ourselves with.

Maybe they have a large circle of contacts - lots of family and friends that are all supporting them, sharing information telling people. If you have 50 people in your corner, that has an impact on getting started. 50 people all sharing your social media posts, putting out leaflets and business cards, telling everyone about you will give you a kickstart. For instance, if your friend is a hairdresser, they have the potential to talk to many clients about your services.

Maybe they got into therapy because of their job. For example, a midwife who sees a lack of support for parents following a miscarriage may train as a counsellor to help those people. They will have a network of midwives, nurses, doctors, social workers etc. that will refer potential clients to them.

Maybe they have money to invest in a beautiful website, advertising, coaching, social media marketing etc. Maybe they have no other commitments and have time to invest in marketing. Maybe they have a background in marketing, branding, tech, or know someone that does which gives them a head-start. Maybe they are an extrovert, or very confident and find it easy to promote their practice and be visible. Maybe they live in an affluent area, or an area where therapy is the norm.

Maybe they live in a central position so appear high up in online searches. This has made an impact on my business over the last few years, as I live 6 miles from the centre of Lincoln and with so many new therapists setting up, I no longer appear on the first page in searches.

Can comparisons ever be helpful?

Yes! Seeing people being successful can be very inspiring and move you forward towards your goals. But for the most part, comparisons don't help and ultimately cause you to feel bad about yourself, and feel resentment, jealousy and bad feeling towards others which in turn can make you feel guilty.

What to do instead

As a therapist, you have better self-knowledge than most, but this is something to always be working on. Come at it from a place of curiosity and compassion rather than criticism. Be gentle with yourself.

Comparison strips us of our individuality, so self-knowledge and really getting in touch with your own skills and qualities will take you far (do the personal statement exercise in the last chapter). You are an individual, so play to your own strengths. If you're outgoing, then network. If you like writing, then blog. If you find connecting on social media easy, use that. Take the path of least resistance, do the thing that you find easiest and least stressful, get really good at that, and then add something else.

I know I'm repeating myself here, but it's so important to keep a track of all your successes, every tiny thing, every small step forward. Consistency is key, so small things done regularly add up.

If you're on social media and see a post from another therapist talking about the number of clients they have, mentally wish them well and scroll past.

Here's the truth about starting up in business. For the majority of people, it's going to take time to get established. You can reduce the time it takes to get known by consistent marketing

Overcome Self Sabotage

using blogging, social media, and making your website attractive and SEO friendly, but it will take time for word to get around. Attracting clients is an ongoing process, and if you are new to being self-employed, then it will take time to learn about starting and maintaining a practice.

So please, do yourself a favour and stop comparing yourself to other therapists, it'll only make you feel bad. Be inspired and uplifted by the success of others because if they can do it, you can too.

Shiny object syndrome

Do you know how many blogs I have in 'draft' that I haven't finished? 23 when I wrote this, I can only assume it's increased since then. How come I went to the trouble of getting them almost written but haven't finished them? Because I was hit by shiny object syndrome.

What is shiny object syndrome?

It's being distracted from what you're doing by something new and exciting. For example, you decide to start blogging, so you learn how to blog and commit to writing regularly. Then someone mentions how well they are doing with LinkedIn. Ooh, well that sounds exciting! So you start planning your LinkedIn strategy, watch a few YouTube videos, and all's well until someone says they are having lots of luck on Instagram! So you abandon LinkedIn and start working out how to use Instagram to attract clients. The result is that you will have been busy, expended lots of energy, but not actually achieved anything. No blogs, no LinkedIn posts, and no Instagram strategy.

This happens a lot to creative people as we get swept along by the creativity of starting new and exciting projects. And it can

Overcome Self Sabotage

also be down to good old-fashioned fear - fear of being visible, being good enough. Because with shiny object syndrome you're really not putting anything out there. It's a form of self-sabotage, and it's very disheartening because it feels like you're doing so much, but you're achieving very little that's going to move your practice forward. You feel tired, exhausted and worn out, and you're still not attracting new clients.

What can you do to help yourself?

Of all the different issues around mindset, shiny object syndrome is the easiest to deal with because there are practical things you can put in place to help you with your distractions:

- Plan, and keep to that plan. We'll talk more about planning later in the book
- Face your fears. What's really happening? Stop, think, take a walk or journal. What's happening for you?

Have an ideas waiting room. A place - Trello, a Google doc or a notebook - where you can write down your ideas as they come up, then keep them safe as you carry on what you're doing. You come back to the waiting room whenever you're ready for something new. This works because writing down your ideas means you don't have to try to remember them or hold onto them energetically, so you can focus completely on the task at hand.

Ponder

When you have a brilliant new idea, write it down and then sit on it for a while.

- Does this *really* feel right for you?
- What are the pros and cons?
- If you do this, what else will you have to drop?

- What will it cost in time and money?

Focus

Commit to only focusing on one thing at a time. I can't stress how important this is. It's far better to just do one thing well than do 10 things half-heartedly. For example, choose just one social media platform to use and use it well, and you'll reach far more people than being on all the platforms and posting in a haphazard and inconsistent way. This gives you a double whammy because it's both more effective and it saves you time

Be clear of your why

Understand why you are choosing to do the activities you've chosen. Be clear on the benefits it will bring you and your business.

Commit

New does not always mean better. There are new techniques, new platforms, new methods popping up all the time, and these can be very alluring, but there are timeless classics that have worked and continue to work that shouldn't be dismissed. Blogging, networking, workshops, word of mouth etc. may feel a bit 'old school' when faced with the latest 'thing', but they have stood the test of time.

I remember when Periscope was the new kid on the block, and it was sexy and fun, so everyone joined. Now, you rarely hear of it. But the blog posts I wrote back then are still here, working hard for me.

What trips you up?

Is there an aspect of what you're doing that always trips you up, like technology? If so, how can you manage this? Do you need to find a technology expert you can call on to help? Sometimes, we just have to pay for people to help us do the things we can't, and it's worth the cost if it's going to get you unstuck. (and it's tax deductible!).

Notice your thoughts

Notice what is happening to your thoughts. Is your head full of chatter so you can't concentrate? Maybe you struggle to remember things? Maybe anxiety makes you feel locked inside your own head and unable to focus on things going on around you? You may not be able to process what is being said or listen fully and take things in.

Our fears can show up in many ways, so stay vigilant and be gentle with yourself. When you learn your processes, you'll be able to protect yourself from self-sabotage.

In the next chapter, we are going to tackle your money mindset and the activity exercise is a warm-up for that. Just allow your imagination to flow.

Activity: Clients and charges

You may not be earning as much as you would like right now, but let's imagine that you were. Write down exactly the right number of clients for you and imagine you have them regularly and consistently. How much money would that bring you?

Now imagine that you are charging more - £10 more per session, then £20, then double your usual fee, then triple. What comes up for you?

Your Growth Journal: Questions for reflection

- How and when does self-sabotage show up in your life?

Overcome Self Sabotage

- What is your normal process for overcoming self-sabotage? What changes can you make to protect yourself and stop this happening?

CHAPTER 9 MAKING PEACE WITH MONEY

What is money

Aah, lovely money! Those little pieces of paper are so powerful! They can bring security, food, shelter, safety, health, pleasure, education, love and life. They can also bring pain, shame, fear, worry, mental illness, violence, suicide, war and death.

Money in and of itself is simply a unit of exchange, a resource, and a tool. However, our attitude toward money is complex, which I find fascinating. Even talking about money is taboo and regarded as vulgar, and people that want more money are very often seen as greedy or bad. Money takes on the qualities of both good and bad.

Think over your client sessions - how often is a clients' relationship with money explored? In my experience, very rarely. People are more likely to discuss their sex lives than their income, debt, savings and spending. Though it should be discussed more, it can uncover some interesting stuff for the clients. As Denise Duffield Thomas, money mindset expert, says:

'How you do money is how you do life'.

Some people are generous with money, some tight, some greedy, some reckless. Some hoard money, too frightened if they spend it, there will not be any to replace it. This 'lack' mentality is the idea that there is never enough to bring you the security you desire. Others are compelled to spend their money before it gets taken away from them.

In our modern cultures, money is essential. Consider Maslow's hierarchy of needs. Money is required to fulfil the basics - shelter, food, water. But also, money is needed for many other things in the hierarchy like health and wellbeing, education, security, confidence, self- esteem, friendships, relationships, respect and achievement. Yet surprisingly, despite money being central to our modern day lives, people trivialise it and say *'oh, it's only money!*' when in truth, money is vital.'

What does money represent to you?

Money helps make our modern lifestyles easier.

When a breezeblock fell off the lorry in front of me, went under my car and burst my tyre (and freaked me out!), money in my savings turned what could have been a major headache, i.e. no transport, into an annoying inconvenience. Money brings freedom and choice.

We get a lot of mixed messages around money. We are shown lifestyles of the rich and famous to dream about and lust after, but also called greedy and money hungry if we want to become rich. A bit like we are shown adverts to diet clubs promising you'll become healthy, confident and sexy alongside adverts of decadent puddings that purr to us about luxury, and you being worth this extravagance. We want fulfilling lives filled with opportunity, freedom and choice, which money can provide, yet the desire for more can leave us feeling greedy and guilty. Shouldn't we just be happy with what we have? It's confusing, isn't it?

Money messages

Consider the messages we receive around money:
- It's better to give than to receive
- Money is the root of all evil
- I'd rather be happy than rich (like we have to choose)

Interesting, as money is completely neutral and neither good nor bad. Money is used to buy goods or services, and we decide which goods or services that will be. You could choose to buy a child a toy, or you could choose to buy a weapon. We inherit attitudes towards money both from our parents and society in general

Consider attitudes towards money in the wider sense. For example, how many films are there where the rich are portrayed as nasty, cruel and selfish and the poor as honest, kind and hardworking?

The importance of money in business

The role money plays in business is vital, because if a business doesn't bring in an income, then it's not a business, it's a hobby. And in the case of being a counsellor, it's a very expensive hobby!

Running a practice costs money: there's room rent, travel expenses, supervision, insurance, CPD, tax and National Insurance, advertising, marketing costs, accountancy and other

Making Peace With Money

expenses and of course, if you are sick or want a holiday, that lack of income needs to be taken into account.

Helping people probably comes naturally to you but asking for money may not. For people in the helping professions, the whole issue of money can become fraught and worrisome. After all, if someone is in emotional pain and you can help, then you should, right? You should give freely. It's a part of being a nice person.

Well no, it's a little more complex than that.

Let's go back to basics: 'what is money?' It's a unit of exchange. You want this 'thing', then it will cost you this amount. Give and take. That's pretty fair, right?

Money isn't only an exchange of physical things, i.e. cash for goods, it's also an exchange of energy, which is important because what we do as therapists involves us expending a lot of energy to our clients, giving our full attention, listening to what's being said, noticing what's not being said, looking at body language, and tone of voice. You are fully 'on' for the whole time you are with them. The second your mind wanders to 'did I get the sausages out of the freezer' then bam, the client discloses something important.

We also hear people. We hear their stories of pain and cruelty, hurt and abuse. We travel with them to the dark parts of their minds and stay there with them. This is hard work. I mean really hard work!

Energetically, we give a lot.

In order for there to be a fair exchange, we need a fair payment for this. Otherwise, there is an energetic imbalance, which isn't good for the therapeutic relationship.

The importance of money in the therapeutic relationship

Issues around money affect everyone, and of course, because we are merely human, it affects us too. We can get really caught up in things like how much should we charge people (or in some cases is even ok to charge people) or is it ok to charge more than other people? Then there's should I offer a reduced fee for some people or a sliding scale?

But the fundamental thing we tend to fall down on is, is it ok to charge people that are in need of help? Let's address this first.

Is it okay to charge people in need?

Okay, I get it, I really do. Someone calls and tells you about their issue, but then says they can't afford the fee and can you see them at a reduced fee? And because you're a compassionate and kind person that only became a therapist because of your need to help, you say yes, which feels good at the time.

But then, a few weeks down the line you realise they have a more luxurious lifestyle than you and turn up in a new car or take time off for a holiday. Or it may not even be something so flash. One therapist I know noticed the client turned up at every session with a posh coffee. A posh coffee that the therapist couldn't afford.

Now, you might start to feel differently, and two things can happen:

- You start to feel resentful and taken advantage of, and
- You feel guilty for being judgemental and angry

Neither of those things are useful in the therapy room.

What is the role of the therapist?

It's our job to create a safe environment to enable change, to explore patterns and, through the relationship, offer compassion, empathy and acceptance. It's not our job to rescue people, we aren't befriending. We *work* with people, and when we work, we get paid.

The drama triangle

```
   RESCUER              PERSECUTOR
 "I'm Accepted"          "I'm Right"


            VICTIM
         "I'm Blameless"
```

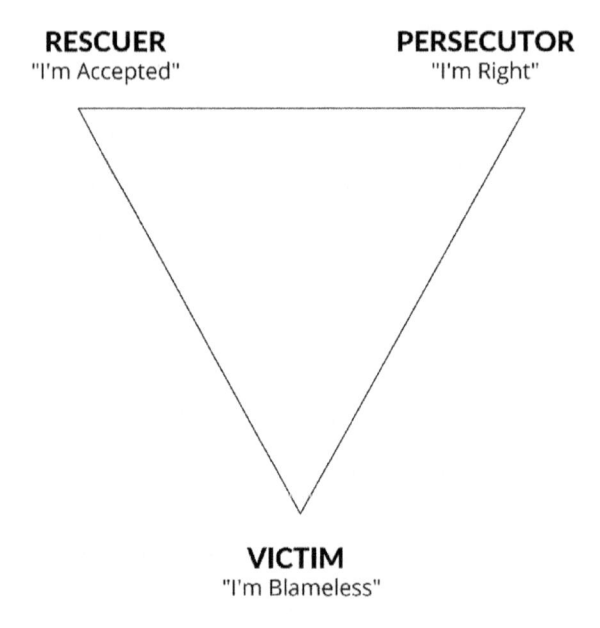

I'm a big fan of Transactional Analysis, and I love the concept of the drama triangle. If you aren't familiar with this, I highly recommend you check it out. But here's the main gist.

The 'Drama Triangle' refers to a model of social interaction and conflict developed by Dr. Steven Karpman in 1968.

It identifies three roles commonly and unconsciously played out in relationships:

- Victim
- Rescuer
- Persecutor

Which are a part of Transactional Analysis games theory.

Victim

I can't cope on my own/I am blameless

The characteristics of a Victim include:

- Wanting to be taken care of
- Not taking responsibility
- Blaming others
- Wanting to be saved or rescued

Rescuer

I have to help others because they aren't good enough to help themselves

The characteristics of a Rescuer include:

- Wanting to solve other people's problems, instead of looking at their own issues
- Feeling guilty or worthless if unable to help
- Often burdened, overworked, and maybe at the edge of exhaustion
- The martyr, enabler, co-dependent

Persecutor

I'm right, you're stupid

The characteristics of a Persecutor include:

- Blaming
- Critical

Making Peace With Money

- Controlling
- Manipulative

We can use the drama triangle to recognise unhelpful patterns and replace them with something new and more useful. We can be in different states with different people and at different times but tend to have a main one. But the thing about drama triangles is, people can flip and switch position, leaving confusion and - yes, drama!

Let's imagine the scenario of someone struggling with their enormous ironing pile.

Victim: <sigh> (victims sigh a lot!) I don't know how to cope with this enormous pile of ironing. <sigh>

Rescuer: Oh well, maybe you can just do 10 minutes a day, every day. Little and often.

V: <sigh> Well I could, but that would mean I keep having to set up the ironing board every time, and that takes a lot of effort for just 10 minutes.'

R: Well, maybe put Netflix on, binge watch a series and power through the lot.

V: <sigh> Well I could, but if I stand too long, I get a bad back.

R: Well, have you considered an ironing service?

V:< sigh> Yes, but I worked it out, and it would cost too much for how much I have.

At this point, one of two things happen:

1. The Rescuer gets fed up that the Victim isn't acting on their amazingly helpful advice and gets angry with

Making Peace With Money

them, i.e. turns into the Persecutor. The Victim is hurt and confused, or

2. The Victim gets fed up that the Rescuer isn't rescuing them properly and gets angry with them, i.e. turns into the Persecutor. The Rescuer is hurt and confused.

This is clearly unhealthy, and it's something to be aware of in the therapy room, and one of the reasons we have our own personal therapy as part of training. It's really important to be aware of our own processes, or it hampers the process for the clients as it's meeting your own needs and not theirs. An honest discussion about your reasons for becoming a therapist in your personal therapy is, in my opinion, vital. We can see how this can play out in our attitude to charging clients.

What part do you play when it comes to charging your clients?

If you are a Rescuer (and many of us are), when someone asks for a reduction in price, you're going to want to help them come what may, even if that means you're not getting sufficient payment to meet your needs.

If you are a Victim (plenty of Victims too!) then you'll work for a lower price but feel resentful, blaming others - your client, the government, other therapists - for you not making enough money.

And if you're a Persecutor (not so many in counselling in my experience, thankfully) when someone asks for a reduced fee you'll not entertain the idea of a lower price and possibly let your disdain at the suggestion be seen, making the potential client feel bad and go on to find another counsellor.

What do you have to do to change this?

Awareness is the first step, as with so many things. Allow yourself to become aware of your stance, and then you can manage it, and you manage it by deciding on your financial boundaries, and then maintaining them.

Decide in advance how much you will charge for your assessment/first session, therapy sessions, and if you want to offer a sliding scale or concessions.

Because if you're not clear about your fee structure you run the risk of unhelpful processes entering the therapy room, and that's not good for you, your business, and it's certainly not good for your client.

Thinking of your boundaries in advance will leave you feeling confident that you can manage questions around money.

Common feelings around money for therapists

'It's morally wrong to charge people that need counselling - they should be able to receive help freely.'

Well, yes, I agree! Therapy is something that everyone can benefit from. I'd like to live in a world where therapy was free for all.

Unfortunately, this world isn't like that. Therapists need to be paid, the same as everyone else, so we either need to be in employment or self-employed. And there aren't nearly enough counselling positions out there.

If you live in a country where there is a national health service, as there is here in the UK, then the idea of paying for healthcare becomes more difficult as we are used to not paying at the point of service. The service isn't free but paying for it is not as obvious.

Making Peace With Money

That can make a difference, both for therapists charging for their service and in the attitude of **some** people that begrudge paying for it.

Kat Love, who works with therapists to create beautiful websites, says:

'Just because the system is broken, it's not your responsibility to fix it'

I couldn't agree more, Kat.

Counselling is a 'helping profession': we help people in need, and it's the word 'help' that can cause us problems, because how can we charge people that need help? After all, you wouldn't 'help' an old person over the road and expect to be paid, would you? No! Because help is given for free. Help is charitable.

If you struggle with charging clients, here's a way to reframe this. Change the word 'help' to 'work'.

For example, on your website instead of 'I help people to manage their anxiety' change it to 'I work with people to manage their anxiety' because what we do is very hard work! Changing 'help' to 'work' is one of those small, subtle changes that really packs a punch. Try it!

My need to be paid is less important than my clients need for therapy.

Both parties need to feel okay in the therapeutic relationship for it to be balanced and work well. In Transactional Analysis, it's seen as

I'm OK = You're OK

That's balanced and equal.

If you weren't paid or were paid too little to meet your needs, it would be

I'm not OK = You're OK.

Which is clearly not a balanced state.

Being paid is a value exchange. The client wants to feel better; therefore, they invest in their health, wellbeing and future life and relationships. It's empowering for the client, it says *'I'm worth spending money on'*. It's an extremely positive statement to themselves and the universe that they are serious about taking care of themselves and prioritising their needs. Let's allow them to feel empowered.

Clients will think I am hard/unfeeling if I charge for missed sessions

They may do. They may not like it at all, but as with everything in therapy, there are always reasons for what we do.

Committing to therapy is important, so client's contract with us at the commencement of therapy. The contract covers several things, including how missed sessions are dealt with. The client agrees to these terms.

Going to therapy and sharing your story, thoughts and feelings is hard. Very hard. The client has to allow themselves to enter a very vulnerable state, and many will push against this. If they had a bad day, feel like crap and just want to go home and work their way through a bottle of wine, the LAST thing they want is to go to their therapist and poke at the pain.

But attending therapy when feeling so fragile is important, and some really useful work can be done at these times. It could be

Making Peace With Money

the first time anyone has witnessed them like this, stayed with them, heard them and accepted them. How important is that?

Paying for a missed fee happens for 2 reasons. You need to have an income, which is important. But just as importantly, to get the best results from the therapy, the client needs to attend.

By allowing clients to bow out of sessions and there not be consequences is doing the client a disservice. This isn't just about money.

Maintaining boundaries isn't easy, but it's important. You can only help the client if they attend, and it's setting expectations about how the relationship will work from the start

I can't charge as much as others, as I don't have as many qualifications and/or experience

If you are adequately qualified in the country you are in, then you have enough skills to help clients and bring about transformation.

Don't underestimate those basic counselling skills - active listening, reflecting, silence, empathy etc. Some people have never told their story or been listened to without being interrupted, silenced or told they are wrong, so being fully listened to is profound and impacts people deeply. Reflecting things back brings clarity, using silence enables clients the space to explore and look deeper, and empathy lets them know they are understood and accepted. Life-changing and life-saving work can be done with 'basic' skills. Don't undervalue the transformative work you can do with what you already have.

As a newer therapist, your learning is fresh and at the top of your mind, which, when mixed with your passion, makes you a force to be reckoned with. You can totally help people and should be paid to do so.

The thing that is truly vital for successful counselling is the quality of the relationship. In a recent survey I did about the public attitude to counselling, someone said 'it is important to find a counsellor who you connect with, I was referred to someone years ago that I just didn't "gel" with and as a result got nothing from the sessions'. You can't learn that connection in a classroom or from a book.

If I charge a lower price, I'll get more clients

Nope, it just doesn't work that way! In fact, the opposite is more accurate. If you don't charge enough, it makes people suspicious - what's the catch? Are you a trainee? Inexperienced? Not very good? Not adequately qualified?

People don't tend to shop around for the lowest priced therapist as they do for other things, like cheaper petrol or groceries. No, in therapy, they equate low price as low quality, high price and high quality, even though we know that's not always the case.

When it comes to counselling where clients need to trust the therapist as they are sharing their stories, their innermost secrets, laying themselves open to you and being completely vulnerable, they want the best quality they can afford, and in life, the best quality isn't usually the cheapest. They don't want to chance it with someone that's not confident enough to charge at least the going rate. I know I wouldn't be looking for the cheapest dentist in town or the cheapest tattoo artist. So charging a low price is going to make attracting clients more difficult.

Making Peace With Money

If I charge a higher price than the average around me, people will think I am uncaring, greedy and only after money

This actually makes me sad. It's damaging on many levels:
- It doesn't allow for people to earn a good income from their practice
- It shames those therapists that value themselves and the transformations they bring.

It's a sign that people consider therapy clients victims that need to be protected and that can't make their own decisions about how they choose to spend their money. (Patronising much?)

What you charge is literally your business and is between you and your clients. Charging for your services simply means that you're exactly the same as every other person in modern society - you need money in order to live.

Money boundaries

Your life will become a lot less stressful if you decide your boundaries in advance and communicate them clearly and simply.

Fee setting

The first money boundary to consider is the fee.

A word of caution: When you're just starting out, it can be tempting to talk about this with friends and family but be careful about who you get advice from.

Let's take my dad, for example. My dad is - well, a bit of a Scrooge. He would literally walk a 6-mile round trip to get milk that's 10p less than the local shop! My dad would never use a

Making Peace With Money

counsellor and certainly wouldn't pay for one. His opinion on what I should charge is irrelevant, so I don't ask him business advice as he's never been either in business or used therapy. But if I was to ask him, he'd tell me I am too expensive.

I've heard many stories of fledgeling therapists having this kind of response from friends and family, and it can be incredibly hurtful and knock your confidence. Don't put yourself through it.

There's more to fee setting than taking what everyone else is charging

You have to take into account:

- Room rent
- Travel
- Insurance
- Tax
- National Insurance
- Pension payments
- CPD
- Supervision
- Professional fees
- Advertising, including directories
- Marketing, including things like website hosting etc

You also have to consider the cost per hour you receive. If you are seeing 10 clients a week, that's 40 hours' worth of fees a month. 40 x £75 = £3,000.

However, you're not only spending time with clients, but you are also spending time on supervision, preparation, note writing, travel, marketing, networking, CPD and accounts.

Depending on your circumstances, you could be spending far longer than you first thought on your practice, and you need to get paid for this time too. £3,000 can seem like a good income for 10 hours a week, but in truth, it's far more time than that. If you estimate all those things take an average of 40 hours a month, then your income per hour reduces to £37.50.

Plus, you have to factor in the time taken for holidays and sickness when you won't be bringing in any income. Also, don't forget to factor in the holidays and illness your client has along with times they might make an appointment and then don't show up.

You can see how important it is to get a decent income for the hard work you do.

Payment in advance

You've had someone contact you and book a session, so you make sure you're available at the stated time, the room is set, and you wait. And wait. And they don't show up, and they don't answer their phone. Bugger!

I see clients at my home so it can be less of an inconvenience, but still, I have in the past cancelled and changed my plans and put myself out to accommodate clients.

But if you don't work from home, it can be more than an inconvenience as you have to get to your room, so you will have extra time and cost associated with travel, along with room hire.

I know and understand many clients are in a chaotic place, and I understand about a clients' anxiety and fear about accessing therapy for the first time too. I know, because I've felt it myself! We need to protect ourselves while encouraging people to attend. It's not okay to always have the cards stacked in the clients' favour.

Many people take payment in advance before the session to secure the place. This serves 2 purposes:

- The client makes a financial commitment to their counselling. It's a statement to themselves and the universe that they are taking their well-being seriously
- If the client doesn't turn up, you won't be out of pocket. But they are far more likely to turn up! It's increasingly simple to take payment in advance, and clients that are serious about attending really don't mind at all.

It has the added benefit of them always paying a week in advance, so if in the future they don't give the required notice for cancellation per your policy, you won't have to try to get payment from them.

Of course, this may not suit you - as with everything, it's your business, your rules, and it's important that you run your practice in a way that's right for you. However, it's a simple system that can save a lot of time, money and stress for both you and your clients, so I highly recommend you give it some serious consideration.

Cancellation policy

Another boundary to consider is your cancellation policy. The clearer you can be about this and then clearly communicate it to your clients the better. Decide in advance what your terms are and stick to it.

Some therapists require 24 hours' notice, some 48 hours, and for some, when clients commit to therapy, they are expected to pay for that slot every week, even if they are on holiday. Again, your business, your rules, as with most things in business, there is no absolute right or wrong, but decide in advance, so you are clear in your own mind.

When I talk through the therapeutic contract with new client's, I make sure to have eye contact with them when I talk about the cancellation policy. I say, ' As long as you give me 24 hours' notice if you have to cancel your appointment that's fine, but less than 24 hours I do still charge, so you need to be aware of that'. I check they have properly heard me by their response. Often, they will nod, or tell me that's fine, or normal, or that they understand. If I don't think they have really heard and understood, I gently expand a little 'so if you can't make it, be sure to let me know, or payment is due, ok?'.

Maintaining boundaries

Setting boundaries is one thing, but there are always those that try to push them. Remember, the boundaries aren't just there, so you get paid, important though that is. No, they are there to ensure the client comes regularly. After all, you can't help if they don't attend.

You may want to consider in advance how you deal with things like severe weather, kids being ill, the car has broken down, a client suffering a bereavement etc.

You could offer online or telephone counselling, for example, if they physically can't get to you. I think there is room for compassion in any business. In my experience, you'll get a feel for the people that genuinely can't make it and those making an excuse.

Clear boundaries help both you and your clients. Unclear and boundaries that aren't maintained do not serve your clients.

Dealing with cancellations

You have your cancellation policy, you've explained it clearly to your clients but then one week, they just don't show up. Now what?

Well firstly, please try not to take this personally, it's not about you, it's about them. Counselling is hard, exploration and change is hard, and sometimes it feels safer to keep those skeletons firmly locked in the closet.

Chances are they are worried that if they call you and say they don't want to come anymore; they'll feel like they've disappointed you or you'll be angry or try to convince them to stay. It will be awkward at the very least, so they run away and hide, and we can all understand that. However, having someone disappear is hard, and can feel personal, even though we know on a head level, it isn't.

But if they Do Not Attend (DNA), they will still owe you your fee as they didn't give you the required notice to cancel. This can feel awkward. We tend to give clients the benefit of the doubt and want to treat them with compassion, of course, but DNA's have to be dealt with,

Here's how I handle DNA's

About 15 minutes after the usual session start time, I text or call the client saying:

'Hi [name], it's Jane. We have an appointment today at [time]. I hope you are okay? If you're running late, I'll see you shortly. Speak soon.

If they don't reply, I send an email to say:

Making Peace With Money

'Hi [name], I'm just checking you're okay, as we had an appointment today at [time]. I texted/left a message. Can you get back to me, please?'

If no response at this point, you need to take steps to get your fee, so I'd send an email saying:

'Hi [name], Unfortunately, I haven't been able to contact you - I do hope you are okay? As discussed in our first session, sessions cancelled with less than 24 hours' notice are still payable, so I attach an invoice for you with details on how to pay. Any problems, and to book another session, please let me know.'

On the invoice state they have 14 days to pay.

If still no response after 14 days, send a physical letter saying.

'I hope you are well? I'm sending a reminder that your fee for the missed appointment on [date] is now overdue. Per our contract, all cancellations with less than 24 hours' notice are payable in full, therefore please make this payment within 14 days of this letter'. Include details of how to pay.

Then, it's up to you how to act next. You could go to the small claims court to get your money, but realistically not many of us do this. This is why counsellors often ask for payment in advance.

Overall, we have to remember the importance of the therapeutic relationship and do our very best to maintain it. A heavy-handed approach can completely shatter that relationship, so handle with kid gloves.

Fixed fee vs sliding scale/concessions

Something else that can cause stress is whether to use a fixed fee or a sliding scale. Once again, your business, your rules, but here

Making Peace With Money

are some things to consider.

If you want to offer a sliding scale, how do you manage that? Some therapists have a scale and let the client choose the amount that feels best for them. If you want to do this, offer a minimum and maximum rate for them to choose from, and remember to have a higher rate than usual too, so people can choose that if they want. So, if you usually charge £50, make the scale go up to £75 or more.

Some people want to offer concessions, for example, for students, people on a low income, people in a certain profession. This is where you need to give very careful consideration to all the options.

For example, you want to offer a discount to the emergency services. Which seems very noble, but why them? What happens when a teacher wants a reduction, how will you manage that? How will you decide who is more worthy of reduced fees?

Remember, reduced fees simply mean you are giving yourself a pay cut. Do you really want that?

Another way people might offer clients concessions is to offer reduced fees for those on a low income. Again, it seems straightforward, but how do you decide who is on a low income? Do you want to see their payslip? Benefit details? Outgoings?

Consider a couple have separated and one party has had to find a new home while the other stays put with the children. The partner that moved out will have to pay rent and start building a home while paying maintenance. Effectively, they have to start again from scratch, and probably would benefit from therapy to work through the break-up, loss and new start. Although they could bring in a good salary, they have virtually no disposable

Making Peace With Money

income whereas their partner could be eligible for benefits yet have more disposable income.

Some therapists like to offer therapy students a reduction if the therapy is a requirement of the course they are on. Again, give careful consideration to this - remember the Drama Triangle? Have you stepped into Rescuer, helping out when it wasn't asked for? Or have you decided their needs are greater than yours, making yourself Victim? It's worth remembering many people train to be therapists at a later stage in life and may already have a job or have factored in their expenses and have savings for this. They don't need rescuing, they've got this!

Saying no

If you are offering concessions, be very clear why and what your boundaries are, and then if someone asks for a reduced fee you'll know what to say. Because setting boundaries is one thing: maintaining them is another - as any parent will tell you!

I don't offer any concessions, I have a simple flat fee that everyone pays, and that keeps it simple. It's incredibly rare that someone asks for a reduced fee, but if they do, I tell them I don't offer concessions.

Saying no can be hard! I actually wrote a whole course and eBook called 'How to say no without feeling guilty or changing your mind', but I still struggle! A glance on Amazon shows you many books all about this, so if you feel uncomfortable saying no or enforcing boundaries, you are certainly not alone.

Here's what I do:

- Be very clear and confident in your fee structure

- Practice saying no. Think about what you'll say, write it down and say it out loud - literally, say it out loud, what does it feel like? Tweak it and say it until it feels okay.
- Keep it written somewhere you can easily access so you can refer to it during a phone call or copy and paste into an email.
- Confidently state your fees on your website etc. I remember on my first website; I stated my fees like this: 'I charge £x (can't remember how much now!) per session. I don't receive any funding or grants and try to keep my fees as low as possible. Thank you for understanding this.' I may have well said 'I'm so sorry, I'm charging a ridiculous amount, please don't be cross with me!'

Ways you can give back without reducing fees

I always say 'your business, your rules', so your fee structure should be what feels right for you, so here are some ways to give back that don't include just slashing your fees:

Decide in advance a number of lower-priced sessions and stick to it. You may decide to have one low priced slot per ten full-priced clients, and anyone wanting a lower price gets added to a waiting list until your slot becomes available again.

You could consider giving a percentage of your fee to your favourite charity rather than reducing your fee or consider offering group therapy. The clients get the help they need at a lower price, but you still get a good income.

Remember, the more you earn, the more you contribute to society. Okay, no one really relishes paying taxes and we all have opinions on what the politicians do or should do with our tax

Making Peace With Money

money, but I think we can all agree that we want better schools, hospitals, policing, social care etc., and earning more money and making a contribution helps our societies and communities. I love the saying 'a rising tide lifts all boats'.

When should you increase your fees?

In a salaried position, generally, you'll get a pay rise periodically depending on your employer. Often this will be annually. We also have to take into account the consumer price index, i.e. how much the cost of living increases over a year. If we don't increase prices, then in effect we are taking a pay cut. There are 2 times when you should increase your prices:

Annually, to make up for the increased cost of living: This can feel awkward for us because we seem to only have fee's that end in a 5 or zero, like £50, £55, £60. I don't think I've ever seen a therapist charge £57. But I say, do it!

Many of us now take payment via card readers that we don't have to faff around with change, and if you don't have a card reader, just make sure you DO have plenty of change. Clients will hardly notice a small increase, but it will make a significant impact on your bottom line.

If you increase your fee by £2, and you have 5 clients, that's a monthly increase of £40, if you're seeing 10 clients, that's £80, 15 is £120 and 20 £160.

An increase of £3 per session makes it 5 clients an extra £60, 10 is £120, 15 £180 and 20 is £240.

When was the last time you increased your prices?

How to increase your prices

When you are at capacity and have a waiting list: You've proved that your marketing is working, and you're getting referrals. That's brilliant! You are becoming the go-to person in your area and getting a reputation for the excellent work you do. People will be prepared to pay more to see you. Yes, this might feel awkward, and you're likely to need to work through some fears or mindset issues that will come up but pat yourself on the back - nice work!

There are a couple of ways you can raise prices.

1. Only charge new clients your increased fee, leaving current clients 'grandfathered' into your old one. However, if it's a long-term client, only do this once: next time you increase prices for new people, raise their fee to the previous new price
2. Put your prices up annually and have this written in your contract. Then remind them two months before the price rise, so they are fully aware.

Remember, opening conversations about money with clients and looking at their financial patterns is great therapeutic work.

Money and self-care - client

People spend money on the things they value and consider important. Some don't value therapy, so it's low on their priorities. However, some value it highly and will budget, use their savings, sell things and change their lifestyle in order to access it. And it's okay for them to do this.

I remember when I first accessed therapy back in my 20's, it was expensive and meant I went without luxuries like new clothes

& makeup and cut back on nights out etc., but I knew it was what I needed to help me to feel better about myself so I paid what I needed to.

This is extremely empowering for clients: it might be the first time in their lives they have prioritised their own needs. It's an important statement to themselves and the universe that they are worth it and are taking care of themselves. They are prepared to do what it takes to make changes in their lives and create a better future for themselves.

Committing time, money and the emotional space to work on our issues and take care of ourselves and our mental health is the sort of self-care that can impact on all aspects of life and relationships for the rest of your life. It can feel good to show yourself self-love in this way.

Money and self-care - you

Things become difficult when therapists are the ones that give, and there is no reciprocal take. Charging clients a fair fee is a part of good therapist self-care.

Because of the very nature of the work we do, therapists are at a higher risk of burnout syndrome, which is defined as feeling emotional and physical exhaustion coupled with a sense of frustration and failure. Burnout is the leading cause of psychotherapists' high rate of depression, drug and alcohol abuse, and suicide.

It's a sobering thought, and one we need to be constantly aware of to enable us to protect ourselves.

One way we can protect ourselves from burnout is to ensure we get adequate financially recompensed because as we've discussed money brings safety, security and choice. Money

Making Peace With Money

enables you to take time off, pursue hobbies that take you away from the intensity of counselling, get help - a cleaner, gardener, etc., access your own therapy. Money can reduce worry and stress. Money gives you choices.

Being properly paid also helps you to feel that you and the service you are providing are being valued by the client.

It's okay to earn money, to have financial security, live well and enjoy life.

Now you have your business hat on regarding money, in the next chapter, we let look at a few more aspects of the business you need to be aware of.

Activity: Money and you

Given we have inherited and internalised so many messages about money, let's take a look at what money represents to YOU.

List all the positive ways money can help you in your life, everything from the basic day to day things like transport and bills to more luxurious, personal things. Don't forget what money brings like security, safety, choice etc.

Your Growth Journal: Questions for reflection

Following on from the activity:

- What day to day issues and problems would having more money solve?
- Which cancellation policy is right for you?

CHAPTER 10 THE BUSINESS OF THERAPY

Running your own practice has many benefits - no bully of a boss to deal with, you choose your own hours, wear what you want, work HOW you want (no more six sessions only).

But in this chapter, I'm going to be sharing some Janey Travis truth talk, because being self-employed is messy and is mainly about trial and error. There will be many failures and setbacks. Embrace them. The lessons we learn the most from are the ones that hurt the most. The trick is to use them to move forward and not throw in the towel, no matter how tempting. Had a bad day? Take a day off, vent, rant and lick your wounds, then come back fighting. It's only over when you give up, and I know many, many counsellors that almost gave up, but came back fighting only to find success and a full practice.

On being the expert

It's been drummed into our heads during training that in the therapy room, the client is the expert so we shy away from the 'E' word like Dracula shies away from garlic! As a result of this, our websites merely hint at being able to help as we're so conscious of being unethical.

The reason we're told to work with a client in this way, i.e. adult to adult, individual to individual, human to human is that in the confines of the therapy room, being an expert can be detrimental to the clients. It can make them feel uncomfortable and intimidated.

But not acting confidently in your abilities *outside* the therapy room is detrimental to your business.

Consider this:

- Would you trust your mental health with someone that isn't an expert?
- Would you trust your innermost secrets with someone that isn't an expert?
- Would you trust your relationship with someone that isn't an expert?
- Would you trust your child with someone that isn't an expert?

Clients need confidence in your skills, and they need to know they're in safe hands.

Many counsellors have told me they are worried about having to sell themselves - they feel shy, awkward or uncomfortable, or they worry about coming across as sleazy or salesy. But it's okay to let people know that you are knowledgeable and can help - why else would they come to you?

The Business Of Therapy

I'm not suggesting that you go around being a self-proclaimed expert! You don't need to. In fact, the more approachable, friendly and relatable, the better. You aren't being a teacher or preacher, but you are offering information, insight and ideas - from one human to another.

Please, let me put your mind at rest: You don't have to sell yourself.

We've all had experiences of overzealous sales assistants or door to door salespeople that won't take no for an answer. They do their best to persuade you and manipulate you into buying something whether you want it or not. But there is literally no point persuading someone to come for counselling that doesn't want to. If by some miracle they do come to you, they'll be sat, arms folded in the chair saying, *'go on then, make me better!'* It just doesn't work. You don't have to do that, so take the pressure off yourself.

What people want from their counsellor is someone that's kind, friendly and warm. This was backed up in the survey I did about attitudes to counselling. Just allow your natural self to shine through, and the right people will connect with you. It's part of the 'Know Like and Trust' factor that's so important in business - people buy from and use the services of people they know, like and trust. People don't like being lectured and patronised.

Sometimes, the best way to market your business is to almost (but not totally!) forget about trying to attract paying clients and simply help people - sharing knowledge and giving information freely purely with a view to helping people. By doing this, you will attract clients, you won't feel sleazy and salesy you, but you make your marketing about helping people. Attracting clients is a rather handy side effect. NOTE: I'm not saying you should never advertise your services, it's absolutely fine to do that.

Personal disclosure

Personal disclosure is another of those things that can send us therapists into a tailspin, so let's take a closer look at this.

What is self-disclosure in the therapy room?

Self-disclosure in therapy is when a therapist shares their own personal views or experience with a client with the purpose of improving the client's emotional or mental state. It should be done solely for the purpose of helping the client and not to meet the needs of the therapist.

Fair enough.

While I totally agree that personal disclosure in the counselling room should be kept to an absolute minimum, I think we should, as private practitioners, reflect on the boundaries we want to keep OUTSIDE the counselling room.

How far should this 'keeping the self private' go?

If you're in an employed position as a counsellor, you can stay pretty anonymous, but as a private practitioner, you have to let people know who and where you are and who you help.

For example, through our marketing, people will see our style of communication, whether formal, light-hearted, friendly and make assumptions about us. They will be more attracted to the one that feels a good fit - which is exactly what happens in as assessment session: you check out a counsellor to see how comfortable you feel with them. In this respect, accurate marketing could save you both time and them money.

In the counselling room, self-disclosure is done only when there is a clear benefit for the client. Outside the counselling room, you have to make your own mind up where your boundaries are.

Sometimes, your niche is to do with your own personal journey, and there may be a benefit for the client knowing that you've been through something similar to them and have a deeper understanding.

Although as therapists we don't have to have experienced something to be able to work with it, there are advantages for both client and counsellor.

I recently read a blog called *'Why I See A Black, Queer Therapist'* written by Steven W Thrasher, a Black, gay man. He talks about the benefits of working with someone who would have a deeper level of understanding of his circumstances. He says:

'Each time I have [posted on Facebook], Black and/or queer friends have enthusiastically reached out to me to ask for the name of my therapist or to seek help in finding someone like him near them.

But I don't know if I'd ever have gotten to a place to talk about these things with a therapist who wasn't also Black and queer.'

If I had gone to a straight therapist, shame about my gay sex life might have more easily held me back. '

You can clearly see the benefits to this client, the therapist and the counselling process. I know of therapists that share their own stories of abuse, narcissistic parents, bereavement, drink/drugs, eating disorders etc. There are times that disclosing can aid the process, start a therapeutic alliance more quickly. This benefits the client and possibly make the counselling quicker, and from a business viewpoint, attract clients.

However, some therapists choose to say nothing about their personal circumstances and keep their personal lives completely separate. I'm a very private person and don't talk about my own personal circumstances in my marketing. However, I have mentioned that I suffer from depression, and some clients say they chose me because they feel I will understand them better.

There is no right or wrong, I have seen both being successful. It's simply about working out where your boundaries are and sticking with them.

Consistency is key

It's important to remember that marketing isn't something that's nice to do or to be done only when you need a few more clients. No, it needs to be done consistently, even when you are fully booked and have a waiting list. I've fallen down here when things have been going well and been a bit cocky, thinking I've got it all sorted. But losing 5 clients over 2 weeks (3 came to the end of their therapy, one couldn't make it anymore, and one just disappeared) soon made me realise the error of my ways. You're looking to always have a steady stream of new client enquiries.

If you are consistent, your results will be too.

Realistic expectations

It takes time to grow your practice to what you want it to be. I've heard people say things like they tried blogging and it didn't work, and I've checked out their website to find, and 3 blogs and 3 blogs aren't enough to gauge whether blogging will be successful or not. As with anything, the more you do it, the better the outcome. If I'd stopped making chilli after my first few attempts, I wouldn't be making the amazingly fabulous award-winning chillis I do now (Ok, I lied, they haven't won any awards, but they are bloody good!). I suspect what they meant was 'I'm worried my blogs aren't good enough', and they gave up before getting started.

There are no quick fixes, no secrets to getting clients and no magic bullets. No one thing works for everyone. Some people report getting lots of clients on an online directory, some get practically none. As we've discussed in chapter 4, comparisons will grind you down. It takes time, so be visible, be authentic, and you will be remembered.

Do you need more time, money and support?

Well look - don't we all?! We'd all like more time, but we all have exactly the same number of hours every day, so we have to learn how to use them wisely. We might dream of having more money so we can have a flashy website, a posh therapy room with a leather chaise (well, I do!) It would be great to have the support of partners, friends and family but sometimes it's just not there.

You have what you have, and that's enough. You can make that work for you. You've heard me say this before: start where you are, use what you have and upgrade when you can.

Your practice is not you. You are not your practice.

I've talked about how our business is our baby and that we love and want to protect it. However, it's important to keep a distance emotionally. Don't allow a set back in your practice to hit you on a personal level. For example, if a client stops coming and you don't know why that's hard and can be confusing. Journal, talk to a trusted peer, talk to your supervisor. Take what lessons you can from it and move on.

There will always be clients that disappear, I'm sure even Carl

Rogers had it happen. Remember, this doesn't just happen to therapists, it happens to everyone in business. People book tables at restaurants and then don't show up, book to have their nails done and forget. Even my electrician friend said sometimes he turns up to fix a customers electrics, and they aren't there - they went out rather than face an awkward conversation.

If you take each set back as a personal failure or worry you said the wrong thing or let a client down in some way, or tell yourself you're not good enough etc., it will have an impact on you emotionally and may start a negative spiral. Remember that failure is both normal and good as it means you are growing.

Being self-employed can be amazing, but it can also mean a never-ending to-do list, no real recognition for the work you do, the frustration of clients not turning up or pushing against boundaries.

Reward yourself often. It's vital that you recognise YOURSELF the work you do and give yourself a pat on the back - but **for the work you do** rather the number of clients you attract. You can't control how many clients contact you, but you can control how much work you do. Recognise and celebrate your wins no matter how small. Acknowledge the work you, and if you keep doing the work, the clients will show up.

Time and money, that's what we all want more of. We've looked at getting more money. Next, we take a look at time.

Activity: Personal disclosure

Now is the time for you to consider your personal disclosure boundaries so you can be clear about what you are comfortable with.

Grab a pen and paper, set your timer to 20 minutes and consider how you feel about sharing:

- Whether you have children
- Why you got into counselling
- Why you're passionate about your niche
- Letting people know your sexual orientation
- Letting people know your relationship status
- Letting people know about personal issues - remember, family/friends have access to your blogs - are there any unwanted consequences there?

Your Growth Journal: Questions for reflection

- What personal qualities do you have that will positively affect the therapeutic relationship?
- What do you specifically enjoy about being self-employed?

CHAPTER 11 TIME FOR BUSINESS?

I was chatting with a therapist friend recently, and we were discussing work. They were at a point where several clients had reached the end of their therapy and left within a short space of time, so they wanted to attract some new clients.

'What do you do to attract clients?' I asked.

'Well, it's time', they lamented and listed all the other commitments in their life, and how they just didn't have the time to work on attracting clients, and I realised they wanted clients, to be a therapist, to get paid but they wanted the clients to somehow magically show up at their door.

This is such a common feeling amongst therapists. There's an expectation that the phone will magically ring with no effort from us, but that's not the way it works. Private practice is a business, and all businesses have to take steps to let potential clients know they are there and can help solve a problem, because

Time for business?

without clients we have no business, and with no one to counsel you aren't a counsellor.

In our busy, busy lives, time is a precious commodity. Ask people what they wish they had more of, and it's time. And money, of course! (Oh, and sleep!) Sadly, I can't magic up a few more hours in a day, but I CAN help you manage it.

How much time do you need?

How many clients would you ideally like to see a week? Let's say 10. But if you have 10 clients, that's not 10 hours of work: it's 10 hours of clients time PLUS admin, marketing, travelling, training, supervision, CPD, research...

You have to be realistic about how much time this will take. List all the activities you have to do over a month in order to be a therapist. I can pretty much guarantee it'll be far more than you imagined.

If you had 10 clients, would you make time for them? Yes! Of course, you would! So, if you only have 7 now, that's 3 more hours per week you've earmarked as work time - plus the extra time for marketing, admin etc.

If you were employed, you'd have a set number of hours you had to work, so make it the same with your business. Work out how much time you need to put aside for your practice and earmark that time. Don't book any other activities in work time, just like you don't in client time.

If you want 10 clients and only currently have 7, that's 3 hours extra to use for marketing on top of their time you usually earmark for marketing. Use the extra time to learn how to market your business (maybe join the Grow Your Private Practice Club) or how to handle technology or get out there and meet people.

Time for business?

Oh, and a word for the technically challenged (like me) - the great thing is, technology companies are in competition to get your business. This means they are constantly making their products more and more user-friendly, and they get easier to use all the time.

Yes, it takes time and energy and pushes you out of your comfort zone but consider how much money each client will bring you: How long do clients usually stay with you for therapy? For me, it's longer-term, so a good average is 12 sessions (if you're not sure, keep a record of the number of sessions your clients have and calculate the average). Then multiply that by your fee. That's how much an average client will bring you. For me, that's £50 x 12 = £600. Surely that's worth making some time for?

If you want more clients, more money and more financial security you have to put the work in. But the beautiful thing about self-employment is the harder (and smarter) you work, the more you earn.

Trade-offs

You can't magically produce all this extra time out of thin air, and if you try to do everything you usually do AND run a business with all that it entails, you will become overwhelmed and burnt out. You are going to have to make some tradeoffs.

This is the reason it's important to know your 'why?'. Why is having a practice important to you? Is it because you want/need the money, you want to help people, you want to have more freedom, to work with people in the way that's right for you? Maybe running a practice will fit in more easily to other commitments you currently have, like childcare. Or maybe you simply want to help as many people as you can to have better lives.

When you're clear on your 'why', then you are better able to prioritise growing your private practice.

In order for you to achieve your goal.

- What will you have to say no to?
- What will you have to delay?

This could mean you have less leisure time, or you have to get up earlier to work, work in your lunch break or work in the evening or weekend. You also may have to budget in order to get money to invest. So ask yourself, is it more important for you to have a successful business or have some new clothes/meal out/coffees? Because something has to change in your life for you to have the space and energy for your practice. Trying to grow your practice on top of all your other commitments will leave you feeling overwhelmed and burnt out or possibly resenting your practice.

When I started out, I budgeted my money and cut back on unnecessary expenses. It's not forever, but it's what I had to do to grow a practice, and it was so worth it!

Time blocking

I'm going to share with you a simple productivity system that will make you more efficient and consistent in focusing on your business priorities. It's called time blocking, and it will make a massive difference in both increasing your productivity whilst also reducing overwhelm.

What is time blocking?

Time blocking is a time management technique that is easy to do and makes you more efficient with the time available. You simply need a diary/calendar, no need for fancy apps, you don't need to buy anything new, just use what you already have.

Time for business?

I've traditionally used a paper diary until recently when I started using a Google calendar, which is free and syncs across all devices, but use what suits you best, it doesn't matter.

How to time block

The first thing you do is block off all your commitments, like clients, another job and childcare. Next, you block off your self-care needs, like doctors/dentist/healthcare appointments, and personal things you want to do, like your children's sports day.

Now, determine how many clients you want and block these out. You may already have clients in your diary, but you can use this to work towards your ideal working week. Consider having set appointment times. I have client slots every 1 hour 15 minutes, which gives me time to write up notes, visit the loo, stretch my legs, refresh the water jug etc. I have 10am, 11.15am etc. and my last one is 6.45pm. (Of course, if you rent a room by the hour this may not be possible.)

Next, block out time for marketing, admin and training. Then add any recurring tasks, like checking emails and social media. And remember to schedule in breaks, as you're far more likely to take a break if it's scheduled in.

Now, when someone rings for an appointment, you can see what spaces you have available and want to fill, which puts you in control. You offer them the 2 most convenient to you 'I can offer you 2pm on Wednesday or 5pm on Thursday, which is best for you?'. If they want a time you aren't available, you now know your boundaries. It's a lot easier saying 'I'm not available then but could do X'. Often people that can only do a specific day or time become more flexible when they can't be catered to, and if you can't, they can find someone that IS able to accommodate them. It's worth remembering if you don't normally work on a

Friday and you bend the rule for one client, that client could end up being long term, so it could mean months and possibly years of working on a day/time that's inconvenient for you.

One of the benefits of being self-employed is that you have the choice to work when it suits YOU. This is good self-care and again, reduces overwhelm.

There is another benefit to this too.

Having client appointments marked in your diary means you'll keep those spaces free for clients. Kind of 'if you build it, they will come', or Law Of Attraction. And this energetically holds that space for them. It says you are serious about getting clients, and the clients will follow.

I've experienced this and seen it happen many times.

I've coached therapists that have a busy schedule and struggle to find the time to do the tasks they agree to, and I ask the question 'so when will you see clients?'. They assure me that if a client calls, they will make time. But the problem is, you will not put your heart and soul into attracting clients if getting them will cause you a headache fitting them in to your schedule, so subconsciously we push them away. Clear space in your diary, don't commit to other things in those times (or if you do, make them things you can easily cancel). Make a commitment to yourself and your future clients to be fully available for them.

What are some of the benefits of using time blocks?

Energy

When I first started in Private Practice, I was so eager that I'd try to accommodate any new client because I was just so grateful to have any!

Time for business?

They would ring, we'd talk, and when it came to arranging an initial session, I'd just say 'so when is good for you'. I found I had clients dotted all over the place, which would often make my life difficult - having to rush home from my other job or work later than I really wanted to.

This means you're wearing your therapist's hat for more time. Imagine you have a client at 10 am one at 2 pm and another at 6 pm. You've only seen 3 clients, so 3 hours work, but you've been 'on duty' 10 am - 7 pm.

This has an impact on us energetically and impacts what we do for the rest of the day. It's hard to swap and change what we do in that way and takes time for us to change headspace, as it were, from being a therapist to other aspects of life.

Stay in the flow

Blocking off time for marketing, writing, etc., means you get into the flow and therefore achieve more in less time.

When I introduced you to the Pomodoro technique in chapter two, I talked about how research has demonstrated that switching from one activity to the next takes a serious toll on productivity. Multitaskers have more trouble tuning out distractions than people who focus on one task at a time.

Also, doing so many different things at once can actually impair cognitive ability. It might seem like a good idea for a busy person to multitask, but the results you get will not be as good, yet you'll still feel tired. This can contribute to overwhelm

Boundaries

It's so much easier to keep clear boundaries and create balance around your work and home life and will create space for marketing - which should always be a priority, but often is an afterthought.

Reduces stress

All those things that seem urgent the moment - like emails or social media notifications are simply tasks that need to be done and can safely be ignored when they pop up because you know that you have time allotted for them at some point in your day/week.

Focus

It focuses your attention. Once you've dedicated time to work on something specific, you ignore anything that distracts you from that activity. When you get in the habit of really working on something for a focused period of time, you'll get more accomplished faster - for example, writing blogs or scheduling social media.

Achieve more

Once you get used to time blocking and you see how much more you accomplish using this method, you'll know that you are working on your most important priorities and that you are actually accomplishing the things that will move your practice forward. No more scrabbling around for snippets of time or not knowing what to tackle first.

It encourages you to make the most of every hour. You'll find that you want to get as much done as possible during each time block. It may even become like a game where you challenge yourself to get more done.

Not prioritising time for your business is a form of self-sabotage, so give yourself time, do the work and reap the rewards.

Time for business?

This book is all about attracting your ideal clients, but who are they? Let's find out in the next chapter.

Activity: Time blocking

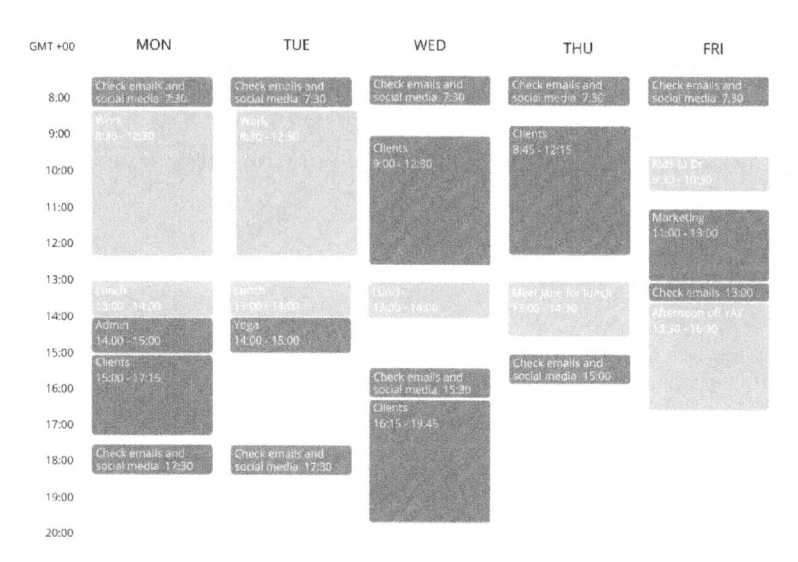

GMT +00	MON	TUE	WED	THU	FRI
8:00	Check emails and social media 7:30	Check emails and social media 7:30	Check emails and social media 7:30	Check emails and social media 7:30	Check emails and social media 7:30
9:00	Work 8:30 - 12:30	Work 8:30 - 12:30		Clients 8:45 - 12:15	
10:00			Clients 9:00 - 12:30		Kids to Dr 9:30 - 10:30
11:00					
12:00					Marketing 11:00 - 13:00
13:00					
14:00	Lunch 13:00 - 14:00	Lunch 13:00 - 14:00	Lunch 13:00 - 14:00	Meet Jane for lunch 13:00 - 14:30	Check emails 13:00
15:00	Admin 14:00 - 15:00	Yoga 14:00 - 15:00			Afternoon off: YAY 13:30 - 16:30
16:00	Clients 15:00 - 17:15		Check emails and social media 15:30	Check emails and social media 15:00	
17:00			Clients 16:15 - 19:45		
18:00	Check emails and social media 17:30	Check emails and social media 17:30			
19:00					
20:00					

Go ahead and practice time blocking your diary. It doesn't have to be perfect, and you can be working towards having set hours, but try it out.

Your Growth Journal: Questions for reflection

- What would having a successful practice mean to you? What would it bring you? What would it bring the people around you?
- Is there something you need to say no to free up some time for your practice?

Conclusion

In this section, we've explored what it's like to be a private practitioner, some of the pros and cons and things to watch out for.

Be aware of any signs of Imposter Syndrome and perfectionism - remember, done really is better than perfect. Keep realistic expectations as getting established takes time and consistency.

Be clear on where you want your own personal disclosure boundaries to be. And remember, it's your business, your rules!

PART 3: PRACTICAL

CHAPTER 12 NICHE

In chapter 3, we looked at having a Seedling Niche, something that's broad, but that will get you started in your messaging and attracting clients. So now we're going to take a closer look at niching.

For authentic, light as a cloud gnocchi, you go to an Italian restaurant. For a banging curry, the local Indian. For dim sum, you'd search out a Chinese restaurant, and for a great Sunday roast, you need a great British pub. Why?

Because they are experienced in making those foods and have honed their skills over years, and sometimes generations. You know they'll have trained, experienced chefs, not someone that knows how to operate a microwave.

You can get Chinese, Italian, Indian and British food - and many more types of food in Wetherspoons, (which is a popular, value pub chain here in the UK), but if you fancied an Indian meal it wouldn't be your first choice - even on a Wetherspoons curry night, because you know the curry you get there isn't a freshly prepared, authentic curry with all the trimmings made by a chef trained and skilled in the fine art of blending spices.

What Wetherspoons IS good for is basic, value food, with a huge menu choice to suit all tastes, from wraps, burgers, steak, breakfast, pies, pasta, fish and chips....you get the picture.

When you go to Wetherspoons to eat, it's functional. The food's fine, but you wouldn't expect many people to take their partners there to propose marriage.

Are you a counselling 'Wetherspoons'?

When someone lands on your website or directory profile, does it read like a Wetherspoons menu? Do you go through the alphabet of issues: Abortion, Abuse, Addictions, Adoption, ADHD Anxiety, Abduction by Aliens etc? Do you offer to work with kids, couples, groups, families, online, corporate, schools, EAP? Think for a moment - what does that say about you?

Remember the phrase 'Jack of all trades'? Do you remember the next line? It's 'master of none', and that's the issue here because people want to see someone that's best suited to help them, an expert, as we discussed previously. So, unless we have a speciality, we're letting people skim our profiles and websites and then move on to the next one, the one that does have a speciality that makes clients feel confident they can be helped.

If you're going to put your story, your secrets, your fears, your mental health into someone's hands, you want those hands to be the safest hands you can find.

If you took my advice in chapter 3, you will have chosen a Seedling Niche, either working with children, couples, working with loss, anxiety, self-esteem and relationships. You can carry on using this broad niche for as long as you wish. However, over time, you might want to specialise in a certain area.

Fears

Although there are clearly many positive outcomes to having a niche, many people put off finding a speciality due to fear, so let's take a look at some.

I don't want to put any potential clients off

Okay, I completely understand this worry: Will declaring a niche actually work against you and make it harder to grow your practice? Well no, it really won't so relax, because there are plenty of people out there needing help.

We're told 1 in 4 people struggle with a mental health problem at some point in their lives. That's a whole lot of people. But look, 100% of people struggle with life at some point, so it's for us to let them, the public know we can help them, and not only with mental health issues.

This fear comes from a 'lack' mindset, which is a feeling that there's not enough to go around. Remember, we looked at this in the money mindset chapter. In this situation, you question whether there are enough people out there for you to have a successful practice. A more useful way of looking at it is 'how can I communicate to more people I can help them?'

For example, imagine this: You love your job, but someone new has started with your company, and they are making your life a misery: They undermine you, they blame you for anything that goes wrong, and they criticize you. This is having a detrimental effect on you and your work. You've gone from being a happy, smiley and helpful person to feeling stressed, anxious and not wanting to go to work. You need help. So, where do you go?

You start 'shopping' for a therapist because you know you need someone to talk to and visit therapists' websites and online directories. But none seem quite right: you don't identify your problem as depression, anxiety, grief, childhood issues... you aren't suffering from a mental health issue.

And then you see:

'Are you having problems in the workplace?

Maybe your boss is a bully, or you have a colleague is making your life a misery?

Come and explore the situation with me, and we'll find coping strategies so you can still do the work you love while dealing effectively with people in the workplace.'

Bingo! Here's the therapist for you!

As soon as someone sees these words, they'll know exactly what you do and who you work with.

'But Jane', I hear you cry, 'that's too small a demographic to be a niche!'

Well no, consider this: what percentage of the population work?

According to a Google search I just performed, in September/November 2016, 31.80 million people were in full-time employment in the UK, which is 74.5% of the population.

How many of them are unhappy at work? I don't know, but just one per cent would mean there are 318,000 people potentially looking for help, and I bet the other 99% of the workforce aren't all deliriously happy in their job either! Remember, this doesn't take into account all the part-time workers.

There's a misconception that counselling is for people with mental health issues, which it can be, of course. But it's also for people that are struggling with life, with relationships, with self-esteem and with communication that could do with some help BEFORE it becomes a mental health issue. If we can make more people aware of this, more people will access therapy. As a profession, if we let people know it's not just mental health issues that we work with, it raises awareness.

Having a non 'mental health' niche like 'workplace issues' takes what we do as therapists and opens it up for more people to access, and by letting people know what we do via social media, blogs, networking, newsletters etc., we are educating the general public to see counselling as a tool which can be accessed by anyone and at any time, not just when in crisis.

Remember the Therapy Rebrand concept, where we are working on encouraging people to access therapy as a form of self-care and a way of maintaining good mental health?

Because as therapists, we don't only see people with mental health problems, we see people that are feeling confused, have been bereaved, are struggling with communicating, suffered at the hands of another, have been bullied, had an accident, or a relationship breakdown etc.

Take me: I have a niche, but only a small proportion of the people I see are within that niche. People come to me because someone referred them to me, through recommendation, they like my blogs, felt connected with me on social media, met me

Niche

at networking or have seen me around. If you become visible and have the know like and trust factor, people will come to you anyway because they want to see *you*.

Just to be clear, we aren't talking about turning away anyone that's not within your speciality: you only have to refer on those people that are outside your capability, just the same as you always have. You can take on any client you want, any situation you want.

Let's look at my niche, relationships with food. Consider for a moment how many people have difficulties with food, eating, body image, weight and size - and I'm not just referring to 'eating disorders'. This comes under the Therapy Rebrand idea too, as 'eating disorder' is a serious issue, but 'exploring your relationship with food' covers so many more things like being on a permanent diet, yo-yo dieting, binge eating, unusual eating patterns etc. Many people can relate to these issues, but not so many would consider their eating patterns 'eating disorders'. Think of the women you know - I don't know many women that aren't affected in some way by this, and there are more, and more boys and men affected too, so let's put a conservative estimate of 1 in 20. Multiply that up, and that's 1,000 people in 20,000.

Think of the area you serve and the population there - I just googled the population of my home city, which is a medium-sized city in the UK, and the 2011 census says 130,200 residents, which is just a central area of Lincoln. I also have clients come to me from urban areas, villages, towns close by and some people will travel further - a lot further when you have a niche.

Maths was never my strong point, but that's a HUGE number of potential clients! Just a small percentage of them would keep me happily in business for years! All I need to do now is let them know that I'm here and how I can help them.

But I don't have enough experience to be an expert in a specific area

Yet. You may not **yet**, but you can already bring about transformation with the skills you currently have. You will get the skills and experience because you'll have focus and direction, so will start to concentrate your efforts on learning more about your chosen interest.

People are interesting and have complicated lives and issues, and as such there is a mountain of information out there with fascinating theories, modalities, techniques, subjects, books, training, CPD, workshops, TED talks and YouTube videos to consume. Learning and CPD cost you both time and money, so it makes sense to concentrate on targeted training that will improve and increase the skills in your chosen niche.

Another thing is, people will literally go the extra mile to see the right therapist. As we've already discussed, people want the best therapist they can get, so are prepared to travel to see the right one, the same as they would when they go to a highly recommended restaurant or their trusted hairdresser. This effectively expands your catchment area. I've had people travel a 100+ mile round trip to see me, and they will for you.

Will it restrict the variety of clients I see?

Imagine you are a bereavement counsellor. Yes, the thing that attracts clients to you is because they are affected by grief. However, what is discussed in work can be extremely varied. Sadness, obviously but also childhood issues, anger, guilt, jealousy, sibling rivalry, historic abuse and family dynamics.

Also, people are bereaved in different circumstances which affects them differently, they respond in a unique way. Therefore, unless you have a 'counselling by numbers' kind of approach, i.e. if your client was bereaved session 1 looks at history, session 2 anger etc., you'll always have variety. Also, you'll be staying up to date with CPD, so you'll always have fresh and new ideas to research and try.

Every individual is just that: individual, unique, with their own story, told in their own way. So, although the loss is what made them pick up the phone, who knows what their story will be?

In the next chapter, I will be helping you to find your niche.

Activity: Who do you really want to work with?

What kind of clients bring you the greatest levels of satisfaction? Start to go back in your mind and consider the clients that you enjoyed working with the most. Why was that? What niche do they fall into? Make a list of clients and consider what they presented, what they really came for and the outcome they got. Look for patterns and then reflect. What does this tell you?

Your Growth Journal: Questions for reflection

- Imagine your ideal client is sitting in your therapy room right now - who are they and why are they here? Why did they choose you?
- What issues do you NOT want to work with?

CHAPTER 13 HOW TO CHOOSE A NICHE

You've decided you want a niche, so how do you actually go about choosing what's right for you? First, take a look at yourself.

Why did you become a counsellor?

The first thing to consider when thinking of a niche is what was your journey into becoming a therapist? Many of us become counsellors because of our own positive experience with counselling, and that inspires us to help others in the same way. You may be drawn to a niche in the subject you've struggled with. It's that fire and passion to help people experience the transformation you did that drives you.

An issue you've had personal experience with could be the ideal niche for you because:

- You have a deep understanding of the subject and issues
- You have greater empathy
- Your passion will drive you
- You can talk with authority

- You will connect easily with potential clients
- You will create content from a place of knowledge

However, what if you wanted to be a therapist after the transformation you experienced, but would find it difficult working with that subject matter because it's too close to home, too triggering?

This may be because you have more work to do on it on a personal level. The work we do on ourselves is never finished. I am in my 50's and am currently in therapy looking at things I didn't have the time, money or emotional space to really unpick until now.

If you couldn't bear to work with something so close to home, that's absolutely fine, you have to consider yourself first and foremost, your self-care is vital, and you can't be an effective counsellor without it. Counselling is hard enough without being triggered every day in the therapy room. You have to be fully there for clients, and you can't do that if you're feeling distressed.

If you're worried about the effect on yourself, then listen to your intuition and choose a different niche in order to protect yourself. You can always change your mind later if you want to, nothing is written in stone.

You may be attracted to counselling because of strongly held beliefs. For example, you may feel strongly that assertiveness and clear communication is a skill that all people can learn and would help people in all aspects of their lives. You may believe this is a skill that should be taught in schools.

You may want to help people to stand up for themselves or recognise abusive relationships. Alternatively, maybe you've witnessed friends/family members going through a situation, and

How To Choose A Niche

there hasn't been adequate help available. Perhaps you have been personally affected by something like suicide, and your passion to prevent suicide may have driven you to train as a counsellor

Many people go into counselling to help some of the most vulnerable in society, and sometimes those people are not in a position to pay for private counselling. The reality is that as a self-employed person, you need to earn a living and you deserve a decent wage, so if you want to work with a specific issue and people with that issue are unlikely to be able to afford therapy, consider how you can work around that.

For example, when I ran the Lincoln Counsellors Network, we had a speaker from a local charity that worked with ex-service personnel suffering from Post-Traumatic Stress Disorder (PTSD). As a sufferer himself, he shared his story about what he'd witnessed in Bosnia and how there was no help for PTSD sufferers on leaving the forces. Over several years, he took to drinking to cope with the flashbacks and nightmares, which got increasingly worse until he lost his job, wife, family, house and ended up living on the streets. Somehow, he ended up in ICU, where he almost died and finally got help. He now runs a charity to raise awareness of the signs of PTSD, and let people know there is help. They use EMDR to help sufferers and offer support in many ways.

Many homeless people suffer from PTSD for many reasons, so rather than work with homeless people, work with them BEFORE life gets to that point. You can raise awareness of PTSD and work with sufferers, so they get help before their life falls apart. If your ideal clients don't have the money to pay for your service, take a look at the first warning signs they need extra help, the step before where they are now - can you work with that?

How To Choose A Niche

Alternatively, once they get back on their feet, can you help them make sense of what happened to them and help them move forward?

Sometimes, we fall into a niche. Perhaps your placement is in a bereavement centre, and you continue working there when the placement ends. You receive high-quality training on grief and loss and become highly experienced in this field. It feels like your niche has chosen you rather than the other way around!

This may be a happy coincidence as you may find you are really skilled and interested in this field. But just because you have experience and training in a particular field, it doesn't necessarily mean it's right for you.

What clients do you like working with?

Which are the client groups you get a lot of satisfaction working with? We all have 'dream' clients: they are never late, never miss sessions, always do any 'homework' and are open and curious about themselves. Yes, we'd probably all love clients like that! But put those clients aside for a moment because that's not the reality of being a counsellor! Those sorts of clients are amazing, but most clients you work with will struggle to access and/or express feelings, or be defensive, or resist change, or engage in 'games', or be demanding, or be suspicious, or be just terrified! This is the reality of counselling. It's hard work, and why we charge so much.

Let's explore what fires you up:

- Maybe you like very intricate work, getting down and dirty into murky pasts and exploring how the past is affecting the present.

How To Choose A Niche

- Maybe you prefer working in the here and now, using a more person-centred approach
- Perhaps you like a solution focussed or CBT approach.
- Do you enjoy working creatively to help those hard to reach clients that struggle expressing themselves, and who's fear makes the process difficult to navigate?
- Do you work well with short term clients, or is longer-term more your preference?

Which clients do you dread seeing?

If we are being really honest, there are going to be a few clients that we struggle working with, and although there is often a great benefit for you in that work, it will make the work harder on both of you, which doesn't have the best interests of the client in mind. Are there any clients/types of clients don't like working with and dread seeing in your diary? When you recognise them, you can refer them on to a more suitable therapist. (Note: This doesn't make you a bad person or a bad therapist.)

Modality

Do you work in a particular way, like EMDR, art therapy, mindfulness etc.? Do you prefer to work with individuals, groups, couples, families, or have an affinity with children, teenagers, the elderly? Is there a particular group of people you like working with, like couples, teens, students, LGBT, disabled, chronically ill, immigrant, adopted, autistic?

Issues you've had the most success with

When you think over you counselling experiences so far, who have been the clients you've had the most success with? Are there any common threads?

Narrowing it down

You should have an idea of the types of people you prefer to work with now, which may be enough. But you may want to niche it down a little further. For example, if you want to work with anxiety, that's a pretty broad field. Who do you want to work with, what issues do you like working with, and how do you want to work? For example:

- I work with kids that have experienced bullying to reduce anxiety and increase confidence
- I work with people that have been in car accidents to get them safely back on the road
- I use EMDR to reduce anxiety
- I work with victims of childhood sexual abuse to build self-esteem and reduce anxiety

Communicating your niche

Most people coming to therapy come because of symptoms they are struggling with, like lack of sleep, depression, anxiety, various coping mechanisms and these are making their life miserable and forcing their hand. They don't realise that it's a shitty relationship with their mum, or abandonment issues from their dad or a historic trauma from the past that is causing their issues and part of the work is uncovering that.

Consider Childhood Emotional Neglect. It's subtle, and not easy to spot as there is no obvious cruelty, but it can affect people for the whole of their lives. Clients just won't be searching for a therapist specialising in Childhood Emotional Neglect because they probably don't know what it is. They will be struggling with the **effects**, so they will be searching for a therapist that deals with that. This could be things like relationship with food,

How To Choose A Niche

alcohol or other numbing activity, lack of sleep, difficulties in a relationship etc.

Often, people won't realise their difficulties are all around early life trauma, or because of having a narcissistic parent and they will likely not really understand why they feel so low and feel confused, probably blaming themselves for being silly, stupid, weak, not good enough etc. It's your job to communicate with them in a way that they will connect with using words clients use themselves to normalise the situation.

Once you decide on your niche, you do The Empathy Exercise (in the next chapter) to really get a feel for your clients' issues and problems, hopes and dreams, and then you'll be able to connect with them in all you do.

Can I have more than one niche?

Yes - and no! If you have two completely unconnected niches, then all your marketing efforts will be watered down, and you may even need two social media accounts for each platform. So you *can* do it, but it will take longer to get established and be lots more work, so I really don't recommend it.

However, you can have two niches that are linked, which makes everything easier.

For example, working with domestic violence and bereavement as two separate areas of interest means you need to produce twice the number of blogs/social media posts, or they will be only half as effective. But if you combine them, you can link them together and call it working with losses around domestic abuse.

You could say ' domestic violence has a heavy toll to pay, and whether you experience it personally, or witness it via your family, it can bring about loss:

- Loss of childhood
- Loss of innocence
- Loss of safely
- Loss of parent
- Loss of opportunity
- Loss of friends
- Loss of self-worth
- Loss of self
- Loss of freedom

AND the confusion experienced following the death of an aggressor.'

By marrying up these two separate areas, you can merge the marketing making a huge number of potential clients. Just a small percentage of them would keep you happily in business.

What if I don't want a niche?

Well, this is quite literally your business, and it's completely up to you what direction you want it to go in. If you really don't want a niche, that's fair enough.

If not having a niche has been a conscious decision, something you have considered and are clear on the possible benefits and drawbacks, then that's fine.

However, in my experience not having a niche is more often to do with fear - that crippling fear that there won't be enough clients, or that you don't have enough qualifications or experience, or that the work will become samey and you'll get bored.

If this is the case, then you're letting fear hold you back, because having a niche is the number one thing you can do to grow your practice and attract clients.

Remember, with a niche you will:

- Stand out in a crowded market
- Attract more clients
- Get more and better-quality referrals, as people know exactly when to refer to you
- Save time and money with focused marketing - drop the scattergun approach
- Concentrate on CPD that will be of most benefit to your clients, saving time and money
- Work with your passions for sky-high job satisfaction as you make a real difference in your lives
- Use your unique mix of experience, skills and training to get better client outcomes
- Speak directly to your ideal client in everything you do
- Become the go-to resource

Could it be fear that's holding you back? If so, do some journaling around this, and see what you uncover.

Remember, having a niche is all about attracting more clients, not pushing them away.

Making therapy accessible

There is a misconception that counselling is for people with mental health issues, which it is, of course. But it's also for people that are struggling with life, with relationships, with self-esteem and with communication that could do with some help BEFORE it becomes a mental health issue.

More awareness means more people access therapy, which means more people get help before a crisis.

As a profession, if we let people know that it's not just mental health issues that we work with it raises awareness that help is available.

Having a none 'mental health' niche, like 'workplace issues' takes what we do as counsellors and opens it up for more people to access, and by letting people know what we do via social media, content, networking etc., we are educating the general public to see therapy as a tool which can be accessed by anyone and at any time, not just when in crisis.

Wouldn't it be great if people accessed therapy as high-quality self-care and a way of maintaining good mental health rather than waiting until they are at a crisis point?

Next, we'll be looking at how you can communicate clearly to potential clients that you're the right person to help them.

Activity: Choose your niche

Choose your niche! It's time for some action, so set your timer for 20 minutes and brainstorm your niche.

Your Growth Journal: Questions for reflection

- Choosing a niche is a very personal decision. How much are you looking to others for validation or permission? Why is that?

- How often do you truly trust your intuition? What's it saying now?

CHAPTER 14 MESSAGING

What I am going to tell you now is important. In fact, it's vital. If you take nothing else away from this book, take away this.

No one wants to go to counselling.

People come to counselling because there is something in their life they are struggling with. Therefore, to attract more clients, you need to discover what that issue is and what they actually want from counselling. Then let them know that you understand their situation and can help them achieve the outcome they desire.

Features Vs Benefits

When it comes to marketing your practice, knowing and understanding the difference between a feature and a benefit is important.

A feature is a factual statement about the product or service being promoted. But features aren't the reason why clients choose you.

Messaging

A benefit is the outcome or result they will achieve.

Imagine this: you've just decorated your therapy room, and you want to put up some pictures. To enable you to hang these pictures, you're going to need to buy a drill so off you go to the DIY shop. You look at the massive choice available and frankly feel a bit bamboozled. Who knew buying a drill could be so confusing! Which of these would you be most likely to buy:

1. The drill that is made of the strongest metal known to man that was designed by NASA scientists glows in the dark, has an inbuilt satnav and has Bluetooth so you can listen to music while you work.

or

2. The drill you will easily and effortlessly be able to use to hang your pictures.

It's the second one, of course, because it will do the thing you want it to, easily and effortlessly.

'People don't want a quarter inch drill; they want a quarter inch hole' Ted Levitt.

This quote speaks volumes; most people don't want to spend their hard-earned cash on a drill. What they actually want is a nice environment for their clients to be in and a simple way to hang their pictures hanging on the wall.

This is the difference between features and benefits, and we can see this in other instances:

- People don't want hot wax to be spread over their bodies and their hair to be ripped out by the roots (feature), but they do want smooth, sexy skin (benefit).

170

Messaging

- People don't want acupuncture needles stuck all over their body (feature), but they do want relief from their symptoms (benefit).
- People don't want to talk about painful things in the therapy room (feature), but they do want to feel happier, less stressed and more content (benefit).

These things by themselves are not things people want, but they DO want the results, and that's why they come. They need your help them get from A to B, and it's your job to let them know you're a good fit. That's what marketing is in a nutshell: letting people know you are there and can help them get to where they want to be.

To attract clients, you need to communicate the *benefits* you provide, not features. For counsellors, the features will be the factual information about your service, which is your qualifications, experience, parking, confidentiality, cost, number of sessions, the modality you work with, etc. Features aren't what make clients choose you. That's where benefits come in.

The benefits a client wants are restful sleep, more confidence, higher self-esteem, to feel calmer, the ability to say no, to enjoy long term relationships, have a more fulfilling career etc.

Often on therapists websites and profiles, I see lists of issues and an explanation of how their modality of choice works, such as:

'...the person-centred approach - also known as person-centred counselling or client-centred counselling - is a humanistic approach. I will facilitate your actualising tendency and enable your personal growth by allowing you to explore and utilise your own strengths and personal identity. I will aid this process and provide vital support blah blah yawn'.

'Yes, but can you help me deal with my bully of a boss?'

When someone lands on your website, directory entry, social media account, etc., you only have a few seconds to let them know who you help and the benefits they can expect to experience. Yes, your clients need to know that you're qualified and know what you're doing. They might have an interest in how you work, what qualifications you have and modalities you use, but those things don't need to be front and centre. On your website, include them on your 'about' page as your homepage is all about connection.

For example, John has been having panic attacks which have been getting both more severe and frequent. This is having a detrimental effect on the quality of his life, and he feels embarrassed by them, out of control and weak. When he's looking for a therapist, he sees:

'Together, we will explore the triggers for your panic attacks, and I'll show you simple, effective ways to manage them, giving you more control of your life.'

He's going to pick up the phone because you're going to give him what he wants: he wants his life back and to stop having panic attacks. He won't be drawn to pick up the phone if he sees a list of qualifications and details of how you work, that's likely to make him feel confused and more anxious. Remember, a confused mind always says no.

What's in it for me?

A simple way to work out the benefits clients can expect to experience after working with you is to ask yourself 'what's in it for me?'.

In this example, your niche is working with relationships:

You: 'I have 15 years of experience.'

Client: 'So what, what's in it for me?

You: 'Being experienced means I bring a wealth of knowledge.'

Client: 'So what, what's in it for me?

You: I can draw on my experience to help you in a way that's right *for you*.

Client: 'So what, what's in it for me?'

How about something like this:

You: I'll help you explore your feelings so you can make the right decision for you'.

Aah, now we're getting somewhere! Do you see how that's more attractive to a nervous client? Benefits might be reduced stress, better sleep, improved work/life balance, fewer arguments, greater intimacy, more resilience, better decision making, improved libido etc. but you'll discover exactly what it is by doing The Empathy Exercise, which I will talk about later in this chapter.

But I can't promise results...can I?

As counsellors, it's important for us to work in an ethical way without making claims or promises about results, and rightly so. After all, no matter how qualified and experienced you are, counselling simply won't work for 100% of people, 100% of the time. We all know there are no magic wand solutions, no guarantees.

However, there's a massive difference between these 2 statements:

Messaging

'If you're struggling with depression, come to me, and I will make you feel happy again', and

'I'll help you to discover your needs and learn how to communicate them effectively.'

Let me tell you a story...

I've had too many nights of Maltesers and Netflix, and I feel a bit sluggish, so I've decided to hire a personal trainer. I know I'm in safe hands because they've trained for years and have a wall full of qualifications to prove it. They know the best, most efficient and up to date methods around, so I sign up to their 6-week program.

My personal trainer is passionate and dedicated, and they motivate me with an interesting mix of something between sergeant major and cheerleader. They spend an hour a week putting me through my paces and devise a 10-minute sequence of exercises to do at home every morning and evening.

But here's the thing: I have to do the work myself; they can't do it for me. If some days I do the exercises at home and some days I just can't be bothered, and then after the 6 weeks I don't get the results I wanted, do I blame the trainer? No. If I didn't do the work, it's down to me, not them. Their program works, but only if I actually do it. Should the trainer stop advertising that you can get results in 6 weeks? No, because it's totally possible.

This story demonstrates two important things:
1. If therapy doesn't 'work' for some clients, that's no reflection on your skills as a therapist. If it becomes personal, you will lose confidence in your abilities,

Messaging

and that will have a detrimental effect on you and your self-worth.

2. If you lose confidence as a therapist and Imposter Syndrome hits, it becomes difficult to market your practice. You have to believe that you are able to help your clients and work with them get to where they want to be. Otherwise, you won't be able to put yourself out there.

If you don't have confidence in your abilities yet, then have confidence in your training, your modality and the skills you've been taught.

You are not responsible for your clients

It's your responsibility to sit with clients, counsel them and be the best therapist you can be, but what they do with that is down to them.

For some, the process is too hard, and they end the work early. Staying with the familiar is easier for them at that time, and change feels impossible. For others, the time simply isn't right, and they don't have the emotional space to engage fully in the process. Maybe looking closely at their life is just too overwhelming at the moment. But that isn't a reflection of you as a therapist.

You may have a little voice in your head saying, 'but Jane, what if it IS me?' sparking up your own insecurities, often bringing you to the ultimate 'am I a good enough therapist/am I good enough?'. But even Carl Rogers would struggle to work with someone that's not ready for change.

This is something to be aware of and work on because there are people out there that need your help, and if you don't let them know you CAN help, that's not fair. You cannot advertise promising results, of course not. You cannot and should not be promising things you have no control over. But think of previous clients, what was different for them on that last session? What positive changes had they made, both internal and external? They felt better about... what? These are things to highlight; let potential clients know what you can help with.

Be clear on your website, be clear in your blogs, be clear that you can offer hope.

The know, like and trust factor

People buy from people and companies they know, like and trust.

If you've ever read anything about blogging and marketing, you've probably been told that to increase the know, like and trust factor you should allow the real you to come through by being vulnerable, sharing personal stories and case studies. Well, we discussed personal disclosure in chapter 10 and know that's not usually suitable for therapists, so how can you stay firmly within your own personal disclosure boundaries while increasing your, know like trust factor?

The know, like and trust factor in action

There's a guy I follow on Twitter who's a man with a van. If you need something moving, he's your guy. All in all, not the most interesting of businesses (in my eyes anyway), but the way he uses Twitter is amazing. When he stops for lunch, he takes a cryptic photo of his surroundings, always making sure his business card (which has a distinctive, funny cartoon van on it) is somewhere in the picture. He then asks 'where in Lincolnshire am I?' And people try to guess. Simple and fun.

Messaging

Also, he plays hide and seek with his business cards. He leaves them in strange and cheeky places and takes a picture of them. If he's in the pub, he'll talk about the top-quality pint and takes a picture, which includes his business card. Or when out with his partner for a meal he'll talk about the lovely ambience, take a picture and his card is casually on the table. His pictures always include his business card somewhere. Sometimes, he hides a business card in a shop, and the first person to find it wins £20. But you never see his face! It's fun, he's funny, and more importantly, it's memorable.

He's been in business a while, promoting his business in the most unsalesy way possible. He will sometimes post smiley pictures of satisfied customers, but only about 1 in 20 tweets are him saying *'need to move something, give me a call'*. So, if I need a man with a van, I know I shall choose him because he has the know, like and trust factor. He's made himself memorable. I know he's likely to have a smile and some banter, and that brightens up the day.

Know: he shares his day

Like: he's fun!

Trust: he posts consistently

I was in a pub once and saw a business card he'd hidden and felt ridiculously pleased, so went on Twitter and reported my find.

Starting a therapeutic relationship

In all modalities, the therapeutic relationship is key. The relationship that develops between the therapist and client over time is the foundation of counselling, and without the therapeutic relationship, there can be no effective or meaningful therapy. Therefore, a part of the initial session with a new client is for them to see if they feel comfortable with you. They assess this not by knowing personal details about you but by getting a sense of you.

In my Therapy Rebrand survey, one of the things that came up time and again was worries about talking with a stranger. By sharing snippets of yourself that sit within your personal disclosure boundaries, you won't be seen as a stranger so they will be drawn to you.

The know, like and trust factor in marketing is simply about letting people get to know you before they meet you, getting the therapeutic relationship off to a flying start.

How can you increase the know, like and trust factor?

Know: Be visible

- Become known for your niche and be the go-to expert
- Include a photo of yourself on your website, bio and social media accounts - don't use a logo as your profile image
- Share some details of your day on social media - a photo of your coffee and cake or a book you've read, for example
- Only share things on social media that fit with your niche, so it's clear what your focus is
- Check out local networking events and start making relationships with other business owners in your area
- Offer to talk at local events or companies

Messaging

- Use live video on social media to let people get to know you
- Share your 'why' on your about page - what makes you so passionate about what you do?
- Communicate with people about what you do. Don't be your own best-kept secret
- Like: Be yourself
- Being kind, funny or warm doesn't cross any personal disclosure boundaries, so think about how you can get that across to people. It will make you be memorable
- Drop the psychobabble, it creates a disconnect
- Allow the passion you have for your niche to come through in everything you do, every blog, social media update or conversation
- Use a conversational style when blogging, write as though you are talking to one person - remember, blogs aren't essays
- Be relevant, use your empathy to consider what your clients are struggling with on a day to day basis and write or share blogs that address those concerns
- Use live video on social media to let people connect with you
- Share something about yourself - your love of Maltesers, of cats, of coffee

Trust: Be reliable

- Allow all the qualities that make you a good therapist come through - your honesty, compassion, acceptance
- Be consistent. Decide how often to blog/post on social media/send emails and stick to it

Messaging

- Only write or share high quality, relevant stuff that your audience will love
- Share testimonials from clients. This splits counsellors - some do, and some don't, but there isn't a definitive right or wrong answer, so consider how you feel about this and make a decision. Obviously, you need their permission and to consider how you handle confidentiality. But a testimonial from previous clients that have had a good experience carries a lot of weight

One of the biggest compliments I get is 'it felt like your website was talking directly to me'. How can you do that?

Activity: What can you do to increase your know, like and trust factor?

Write out what you might say when meeting someone for the first time. Then stand in front of the mirror and say it. What do you notice about your body language? Next, record yourself. Watch and listen back. Again what do you notice? Would you like and trust you?

Your Growth Journal: Questions for reflection

- Consider your process for buying a product or service, what (other than price) makes you buy?
- What companies do you trust? Why?

CHAPTER 15 THE EMPATHY EXERCISE

Often in business, we are encouraged to do an Ideal Client Avatar exercise where we imagine who our ideal clients are, what they look like, where they live, and how they live their lives. This includes things like what car they drive, what books they read, what colour hair they have. But I have never found this a particularly useful exercise because who cares what car they drive or what colour their hair is!

In this chapter, we're going to take a look at a simple way of really getting into the heads of your potential ideal clients and get a better understanding of:

- Their issues and problems
- Their wants and needs
- Their hopes and dreams

This is such an important exercise as it enables you to let potential clients know that what you are offering is what they

The Empathy Exercise

need. Not only that, it's playing to our strengths, as we tend to have lots of empathy which makes this a highly effective exercise.

Instead of creating a made-up person, think of three real people that would be ideal clients for your niche. These could be previous clients that you've loved working with, someone you know, maybe a friend, family member or colleague that is struggling with the sorts of issues you work with. Or it could even be a character from TV or film.

Now turn off all your distractions and set a timer, we're going to do a 5-minute Pomodoro for each one. Now pretend you are one of these people. Imagine a day in their life and take some time to really feel like them. Pretend you are playing them in a film, and you need to know them inside out. Close your eyes if it helps.

Then, write about their day. How do they feel when they wake up? What is their morning routine like? Do they work? Stay home with kids? Care for someone? How do they spend their lunchtime? Who are they around in the day? What are their relationships like? How do they spend their evening? Do they have a partner? Social life? How are they feeling? If someone asks how they are, what might they say? What is their bedtime routine? How well do they sleep?

What would stop them from coming to counselling?

Consider their pain points:

- What's keeping them up at night?
- What's their biggest frustration?
- What's the one thing they most want to change?
- What thoughts are ruminating in their head all day?

The Empathy Exercise

- What are their fears?

How would your ideal clients describe their issues, what words are they likely to use? You could even join a Facebook group for topics in your niche and pay close attention to the language people use when talking about the problems they face.

Now start again and go through the whole exercise of how their day is AFTER they have had successful therapy. What has changed? How do they feel? What will they be, do or have as a result of their successful counselling?

This is where we as counsellors can fall down, because we are extremely good at understanding their pain points but less good at identifying their hopes and dreams, but if you want to create that connection, this is vital.

Their ideal outcome:

- How will their life be different?
- What becomes easier for them?
- What has changed in their relationships?
- What have they stopped doing?
- What have they started doing?

When the timer goes off, stop. Take a 5-minute break and repeat for the other two.

Compare your findings. What things are commonalities? For example, maybe all of them struggle with sleep. Mark all the similarities, and use these within your main messaging on your website homepage, directories, social media bios etc.

All the other things will make great subject matter for social media and blogs. So, if one of them feels stressed on their morning commute, for example, you can post or blog about podcasts, mindfulness apps etc.

Don't make this hard!

This isn't about writing an essay so please don't do that! And it most certainly doesn't have to be perfect. All we are doing is getting the knowledge you already have in your head out, so just a brain dump. This can be added to if you have something new pop up.

When you've done this exercise, imagine that whenever you are writing, whether that's on your website, blogs or social media etc., you are talking directly to one of those three people. Imagine writing them a letter or a personal email. Imagine how you'd talk to them over a coffee, what words would you use? This will keep your writing conversational and relatable, and your ideal clients will read them and think to themselves 'this person really gets me'.

In the next chapter, we will look at what you need from a website.

Activity: The Empathy Exercise

Do The Empathy Exercise, and keep adding to it as new things pop into your head.

Your Growth Journal: Questions for reflection

- What would stop your ideal client from coming to counselling?
- How would your ideal clients feel about seeing a counsellor?

CHAPTER 16 WEBSITES

I remember my first website. It made me feel like a proper grown up like I was a *real* counsellor, and I felt like the bee's knees! It had some pretty pictures, and I talked about how passionate I felt about helping people, what qualifications I had, and it had the 'a-z' list of issues counselling helps with - you know the one, abuse, addictions, adoption, ADHD anxiety, abduction by aliens etc. I thought it was THE BEST THING EVER!

But when I look back at it now, I smile, and it makes me realise just how far I've travelled. I made every single mistake going! My website was all about me, it didn't speak to potential clients, and I didn't have a niche back then, so I was trying to attract everyone and as we've discussed in previous chapters, try to attract everyone, and you attract no one.

People often ask me whether a website is absolutely necessary, and I say yes, it is. It's not the first thing you should do - hell, it's not even the second or third! But at some point, you will need one. You know yourself when you are looking for a product or service chances are you'll fire up Google and check out what's out there first.

There's always that one person that says they built their practice to capacity without ever having a website. I'm sure that can be done, but I know when I started out, when I was a single mum with 2 young kids, one with a medical condition. Back then, I really didn't have the time to wait for word of mouth or referrals to start bringing me clients, and I certainly didn't have the money for a lot of paid advertising. I needed to take a more proactive stance and get known.

Your website is your shop front, your online home and does a lot of heavy lifting for you. The role of your website is to let your ideal clients know that you are exactly the right person to help them, and you do this through the copy (the writing on the website) branding - colours, fonts, images and other messaging like content marketing, e.g. blogging, podcasts and video.

NOTE: A good website is a must - in this day and age we should all have an online presence - but don't let not having a website stop you from getting started, go check out the 'putting down roots' section in the quickstart guide

It's not about you

When people are looking to access therapy, they aren't interested in you - at least, not initially. All they are thinking is 'can you help me'. Your job is to let them know that you CAN help them.

If they land on your website and it's all about you, your qualifications, why you trained as a counsellor and what modalities you feel passionate about, they will simply click away. Remember, the reader is just thinking 'what's in it for me?'. Take a look at chapter 14 for more on this.

Branding

'Branding is deliberate differentiation.' Debbie Millman

Branding is all about what you are known for or seen as. Branding is a massive subject all by itself, and there are many books devoted to it, so please check them out if you want to look more closely at this. However, most of us, as therapists are running a small business, not international companies, so we simply want a cohesive, attractive look that appeals to our ideal clients.

Consider your overall style. What do you think will be most attractive to your ideal clients? Remember, it's all about them. Will they like minimalistic, natural, light and airy, comfy cosy, maybe something more spiritual?

You need a style that will stand out as yours, so when people see your posts on social media etc. it is instantly recognisable. You can do this by deciding on a colour palette, fonts, image types and designing simple templates

Do some research and check out other websites for inspiration. You could check out other therapy websites, but I'd say just look at other websites generally, and a great place to do this is Pinterest. Consider what you like and what you don't like.

Branding can be such fun because you get to let your creative side out to play. However, it's so easy to get stuck here because there are so many choices. And I know, as I have spent many a happy hour choosing between one shade of orange and another slightly different one. Yes, you want it to look right, but choosing exactly the right shade won't make any difference to your ability to attract the right clients.

And while we're on the subject, a word to the wise: you can spend hours, days, weeks on this and it can become an exercise in procrasti-branding, so give yourself a time limit. Set a timer, and allow one Pomodoro for colours, and one for fonts. I say this as I have spent so long on these things in the past and I now realise it was a form of perfectionism and procrastination for me. I could tell myself I was working on my business, but really, I was hiding, doing 'busy' work that was fun which put off the inevitable but scary part of actually getting out there and being visible. As I said in the self-sabotage chapter, be aware of your processes so you can protect yourself.

It's exactly the same with logos. Basically, for the majority of therapists, you don't really need one, especially when you're first getting started. I've seen people take so much time, money and energy trying to design the exact right one or spend money that would be better spent in other areas of your business. You don't need a fancy logo, and you certainly don't need an expensive one: you can upgrade in the future if you want to.

What pages do you need?

Most of us only need a 5-page website to start, and you can add more as and when you need to, so to get started I recommend:

- A homepage
- About me page
- A page for content like blog, podcast or video
- FAQ (Frequently Asked Questions) page
- A contact page.

Let's take a look at each of these:

Homepage

Your homepage is your shop window, so here's where you want to really connect with your visitors.

First Impressions. In our busy, noisy lives people have very short attention spans, and when someone lands on your website, you have about 7 seconds to catch their attention, or they will simply click away, so you're aiming for people to land on your website and think 'OMG this person really gets me'.

Put yourself in your potential client's shoes and imagine you are visiting your website for the first time. What do you see?

The space people see when they first land on your website is prime real estate, so ask yourself - is it immediately clear what the site is about and who you work with?

A common mistake is wasting this space, and it's taken up with the logo, navigation and an image. These things don't speak to the visitor, they don't connect with them and compel them to keep looking.

If you have a logo, keep it small, and I recommend choosing a nice big uplifting image which shows hope and having a tagline over the image which will speak to the reader and let them know you understand them.

For example, imagine you work with children, and on your homepage, there is an image of a child laughing and written over the image:

'You want the best for your child... so do I.'

Anyone looking for help for their child will feel drawn to you and keep reading your website.

But a word of warning: a tagline is another thing you can worry about and spend a lot of time on. Again, I recommend doing this in a very time-limited way - just a 10-minute Pomodoro to do a brainstorm. Remember, this isn't written in stone, you can change and amend at any time.

Here are some more ideas:

- Feel anxious? I can help
- Counselling for men: because men need support too
- Communication, simplified
- Support when you need it
- Helping you make sense in a crazy world
- Helping couples communicate
- Because it's never too late to start again
- Breakthrough your anxiety roadblocks

Write your homepage using information you gleaned from The Empathy Exercise. You need to address clients pain points, i.e. the issues they are currently struggling with, and also their ideal outcomes. Let them know you can help them (and if this worries you, read more about this is the 'messaging' chapter).

Include a short section introducing yourself with a photo of you and a 'read more' link which directs them to your 'about' page. People will be coming to see *you*, so always have a picture of you. Yes, even if you're shy. They want to picture who will open the door when they come to their first session, it takes away anxiety and anyway we can remove blocks is good.

Include any 'social proof' like radio interviews, inclusion in publications, guest blogs you've written. You can share the logos of those here, and if you take testimonials, share them too.

You might want to share some of your content - your blogs etc. You want to let them see that you offer lots of help and guidance freely and direct them there. This is great because the more they look around your website, the more likely they are to contact you or remember you, but also it decreases your bounce rate. Your bounce rate tells the search engines like Google how long someone stays on your website. If people spend a while looking around your website, Google thinks 'Ooh, this must be interesting, I'll show this website to more people that do a similar search'.

Finish your homepage (and every page) with a Call To Action (CTA). The CTA guides them to their next action, maybe contact you, read a blog, read your FAQ's. Include just one CTA per page. It could be 'Contact me now for a no obligation 10-minute call' and a link to your contact page, or 'check out my blogs on [your niche]' and link to your blog page.

About page

Again, this isn't about you! It's still about how you can help the potential clients, so don't rush in with all your details, that comes later.

In the first part of the page, use more information from The Empathy Exercise to let them know that you understand them. Talk more about their issues, and (importantly) what they want their life to be like when they are free from these issues. Give them hope.

Now, finally, you can talk about you. Now is your chance to shine. Consider your personal disclosure boundaries and share what you're comfortable with about what brought you into counselling and your niche. Allow your passion to show. Then add details of your qualifications and experience. Include logos of membership bodies you belong to, where articles have been published or where you have given interviews or spoken publicly.

Add testimonials if you collect them and remember to end with a CTA. If they have read to the end of your about page, they are probably quite serious about wanting to access help, so your CTA at the bottom of the about page should always be to contact you, with a link to your contact page and also your phone number.

Blog

This is the place you house your blog posts, podcasts or videos. We will be looking at content production later in the book, but for now know that if you have a website, you'll want a place for your content.

FAQ

Do you remember the first time you had counselling? I do, and I was pretty damned terrified, suspicious of the process and felt very vulnerable. I had no idea what to expect or what would be expected of me. I even thought there was a secret camera, and the session would be filmed for the therapist to watch later. I don't know where that idea sprang from, but it was there! Anything you can do to let potential clients know what to expect is good, and one way of doing that is a Frequently Asked Questions (FAQ) page on your website.

The FAQ page should answer questions in a very short and concise way, it's not a place for lengthy explanations. They should find their answer quickly and easily. However, if you've written a blog which would offer a fuller explanation, add it - or write one! - and link to it.

Although these are pretty factual and should be short and concise, let your warmth come through in the answers you give. You could include things like:

1. Making an appointment

If a client wants to make an appointment with you, spell out how the process works. Should they ring? If so, you might want to reassure them that your voicemail is confidential. Check out the section regarding voicemail below. Should they email? What do you need to know? What happens next? How soon can they expect a reply from you?

2. Price and payment

Obvious maybe, but make sure your prices are available and clear with what methods of payment you accept? Do you require payment in advance? Do you offer concessions (remember we talked about this is the money mindset chapter) and if you do, what are they? Set this out clearly, because some anxiety around asking could be enough to put people off. Remember, a confused mind always says no.

3. Availability

What days/hours do you work?

4. The number of sessions (optional)

Obviously, this isn't something you can predict, but I like to mention it, so they know we'll look at this on meeting. I say 'the number of sessions varies enormously and depends on what issues you bring, and we will discuss this at your first session'.

5. Directions and Parking

These details can go a long way to calm nerves before a first meeting. Be as clear as you can with directions, and consider embedding a google map.

Where can they park, and will they need change for parking? Is there an entry system? Are you on a bus/train/tube route? A photo of the exterior of your building can help.

Mention if you do or don't have disabled access or use of toilet facilities.

6. Confidentiality

Don't let this become a lengthy explanation. I say 'I take your confidentiality very seriously, and this will be discussed with you at our first meeting'. This reassures them that you will cover this fully when you meet.

This page is called a 'Frequently Asked Questions' page, so if you notice the same question being asked repeatedly, then add it here. For example, you might briefly outline the process of your first counselling session or advise how to get the most from counselling. You could also write a blog to cover this, and link to it.

Consider this: If you work with children, what would a parent want to or need to know? If you work with couples or groups, what do they want to or need to know? Maybe you run an online counselling practice, so what are the questions your potential clients need answering?

Contact

The contact page is probably the most simple page on your website. It will include a contact form where people can email you directly from your website, along with your phone number and a short message to encourage people to contact you.

Voicemail

Let's talk a little about voicemail messages.

Websites

Imagine this: You're feeling troubled and need some help, so you browse the web to find a local therapist that you like the look of - one that has experience in the issues you're dealing with, one that seems approachable and warm. You've kept the number in your diary for a couple of weeks, and every time you go to dial the number you put the phone back down again, hands shaking until finally, you pluck up the courage to ring and make an appointment. Nervously, you dial the number...

Ring ring.

No answer. Oh. Or...

Ring ring

No answer, then generic mobile phone voicemail message. Oh!

Do you leave a message, not really knowing if your confidential, personal message will get to the right person? Well, I wouldn't! No, you feel let down, and go to the next person on your list.

Your client is looking for a safe, trustworthy and confidential place to go and talk through their difficulties, and it's your job to provide that. They need to know that if they leave a voicemail message, it's safe and will reach only the right person.

You work hard to get clients:

- You craft the perfect bio on directories
- You advertise
- You blog
- You use social media
- You network

Which all take time, money and effort. It makes sense that when clients want to use your services - which for some people takes a whole lot of courage to pick up that phone - you provide an amazing experience for them.

Here are some ideas to make a great first impression:

1. Have a dedicated phone just for your business

It's not expensive to get a separate mobile phone, and a SIM only deal which means your voicemail message can be specific to your private practice. This has the added bonus of making it easy to 'switch off work' for the day and achieve a better work/life balance. Or if you still have a landline, keep it just for work.

2. Be mindful of your voicemail message

You need to confirm they've reached the right place, that the message will be confidential (make sure it is) and what you want them to do next. I like to make sure they leave their number, even if they think I already have it as it saves me having to go search it out.

Depending on your niche, you may wish to include instructions on what to do if they're in crisis, like visit their doctor, call The Samaritans or go to the emergency department of their local hospital. Here's an example of a voicemail message to record:

'Hi, you've reached the confidential voicemail of [your practice name].

I'm unable to answer your call at the moment, but if you leave your name, phone number (even if you think I already have it) and a short message I'll return your call as soon as possible.'

First impressions count, so you want to sound both warm and professional. When you record the message, stand up (this will make you sound more confident) and smile (this will soften the voice and make you appear warm).

3. Check and reply

Some clients will have a shortlist of people they want to call, so you may not be the only one they are considering. Therefore, make sure you check your messages and reply as soon as you possibly can. It's frustrating to discover you've lost a client because you weren't quick enough to get back to them.

4. Use a service

If you are working full time and don't want to miss your calls, consider a call answering service. Basically, it's like having a receptionist to answer your calls and take messages. There are many services out there at all different price ranges, and some are specifically for health service providers and so have a better understanding of the need for confidentiality.

5. Password protect your voicemail

Give an added layer of protection to you and your clients by adding a password to your message.'

DIY Vs Done for you

When it comes to creating your website, you have two options:

- Have it made for you
- DIY, and make it yourself.

There are arguments for both of these, so let's take a closer look.

Whether doing it yourself or employing a professional, before you get started brainstorm what you want it to look like, what you want to say and think about what your website is going to need. A simple and effective way of doing this is to sit down with paper and pen and actually do a rough drawing of how you want the pages to look. Research websites to see what you like, don't like, definitely need and features that are optional. Write it all down.

Now write the copy (words) for each page. It doesn't have to be perfect, and it can be changed at any time, so don't get too hung up on it. No matter how much time you spend on it, in 6 month's time, you'll probably want to change it anyway, that's just the way it goes! Also, consider what images you want for your website. My recommendation is they are uplifting and give hope for a brighter future.

There's more to a website than how it looks, you also have to consider site speed (how fast it loads when someone clicks on it), user experience (how easy is it to navigate) and site security. And a responsive website - one that looks good both on a computer, tablet and mobile - is a must.

Done for you

There are obvious benefits here. You speak to a website developer about your wants and needs, and they will produce a good looking and functioning website. This is perfect if you are a technophobe as it takes away the techie headaches for you. Yes it will cost more, but it's just the cost of running a business and let's face it - you're a therapist, not a web designer. Your website is important, you want it to look good and work well. That said you can get a good, solid website done relatively inexpensively, you certainly don't have to spend thousands.

Websites

Paying to have your website built is a wise business investment. The Return On Investment (ROI) will be high, the extra clients it can attract will more than pay for its cost. Rather than managing the stress of trying to wrangle a website, you'll be free to work with clients and do other marketing activities, which is a better use of your time and energy and bring in the funds to pay for your website.

When looking for a website designer, ask for recommendations BUT make sure people aren't only recommending their friends and family. Very often, a web designer has a portfolio of websites they have designed on their own website, so pick the phone up and ask the business owner about their experience. I tend to go for neither the cheapest nor most expensive options.

Don't leave everything in the hands of the designer, as the chances are they don't know what therapists do. We have to attract clients in slightly different ways than other types of business. I've seen websites where therapists have left the design and copy in the hands of the designer, and they simply haven't been appropriate. Their job is to make a good-looking website that works. Your job is to make sure it's the right website for you, that will use your voice to attract clients. Stay in control.

Before you employ someone, get a contract and read their terms and conditions. Be sure to ask about how to make changes to your website, for example, how to add new blog posts and tweak the copy. This will make a massive difference for you going forward as you won't have to wait for someone else to make any changes for you. Some developers charge for any changes like this so be sure to check this out with them in advance

Many developers will go through how to use your new website and the process of making changes with you. Some may provide simple training, and some make videos. Be sure to check at the start what training is included.

Websites have to be updated from time to time - a bit like updating your laptop or apps on your phone, so check the process: do you do it, or do they?

Finally, ask if there are any further costs you need to budget for.

Doing it yourself

If you're comfortable finding your way around technology, it's getting more and more simple to make your own website. The technology is becoming ever more easy to use, and it's possible to build and run a website for less than £5 a month, so it's definitely the cheaper option.

But there is more to creating a website than making it look pretty. It also needs to be quick, be protected, be easy to navigate and be SEO optimised. If you've never done this before, be sure to give yourself plenty of time as it's likely to take a lot longer than you anticipate as everything will be new to you. You don't have to launch your website right away, you can work on it in the background in stages, maybe week 1 set it up, week 2 work on the homepage, week 3 the about page etc.

Check that the platform you use has robust customer support for those times you need help.

Map your site out, plan it in advance and test it all works before going live. Your website should be all about your ideal clients, so use your findings from The Empathy Exercise to make that connection. When it comes to the copy, clear beats clever every time.

Websites

You can demonstrate that you understand and can help:

- With blogs addressing their issues
- With copy that talks in their language
- With images that resonate

The role of your website is to let your ideal clients know that you are exactly the right person to help them.

Now you have a website, you have a place to house your content, so in the next chapter, let's take a look at what content actually is, and how it helps you attract clients.

Activity: Make yourself a branding style sheet

Check out some websites for inspiration, and then grab some paper and pens, and plan out your web pages. Then make yourself a simple branding style sheet.

A simple colour palette has 5 colours:

- Main colour
- Highlight - to use on buttons and anything you want to stand out
- Accent 2-3 shades/tones to go with your main colour

And 3 fonts:

- A heading
- A subheading - most often a script style (make sure it's easy to read)
- Body - for your main text

You can then use these colours and fonts on everything you do. - your website, blog images, social media etc. This looks professional, people will start to recognise your style, and you'll be remembered.

Your Growth Journal: Questions for reflection

- How can I find more money to have a website built? E.g. sell things on eBay, cut back on luxuries etc.
- How can I find the time to build a website?

CHAPTER 17 SEARCH ENGINE OPTIMISATION (SEO)

SEO - this is for website experts and techy people, isn't it? Well, no! SEO is one of those things that sounds really techy - I mean, it's an acronym, for God's sake. Surely that means to do it you need an extra qualification?! Well, you don't. SEO is one of those things we may shy away from, but actually, a basic knowledge and understanding will get you far.

What is SEO?

Imagine Google is an enormous library with millions of websites, web pages, blog posts, online shops etc. When we go to Google and type a question like 'can people get addicted to Maltesers?', Google has to have a way to search through everything online and bring you answers that match your search, so it will search for things that have the words 'Maltesers' and 'addiction'. When I tried this just now I got these top results:

- Malteser addicts 10 stone transformation

Search Engine Optimisation (SEO)

- 'Addicted to Maltesers', a question in a forum
- 'How to beat Food Addiction'
- 'How do you stop eating Maltesers?'

Well done Google, you did good!

Search engines look for keywords and key phrases in my question to search for what I want to know. Using those keywords, Google uses magic to find the most relevant matches to answer my question. What we need to know about SEO as private practitioners is, we need to tell Google what our website and our web pages are about, so they will be found in searches.

A keyword could be something like counsellor, therapist, psychotherapist, anxiety depression

A Key phrase could be counsellor in Lincoln, anxiety therapist London, couple's counsellor Manchester.

Or for blogs, '7 ways to get more sleep' or 'how to improve your self-esteem'.

When we talk about SEO, all we mean is 'will Google know what this site/page/blog is about so it can show us in search results?'.

As I say, basic knowledge is enough to make a massive difference, there's no need to employ an SEO company - and incidentally, when people email or call saying they can get you on page 1 of Google beware because nobody can promise that.

When you write blog posts, you can name them with this in mind and use the most relevant keywords or key phrases in the title and a couple of times in the post.

Another simple way of increasing your SEO is to properly name your images, so if you use a photo of your lovely therapy

Search Engine Optimisation (SEO)

room on your website, it will probably be named IMG 746352. You can change that to 'Jane Travis relaxing therapy room in Lincoln' and add that to the alternative (or alt) text box on your website.

There are regular changes in SEO best practices as search engines change regularly, so I recommend following an SEO expert on social media to stay up to date.

How your website platforms helps with SEO varies from provider to provider, so check what training and information your website provider provides.

The bottom line is, SEO isn't a dark art, it's just about making sure search engines show you to the right people. Read up on it, do your homework and find out how to optimise your website and blogs and don't worry about employing an SEO expert on a monthly retainer, although a one-off session with an expert may be helpful.

Also, you don't have to learn all this now, it's definitely something you can pick up and learn more about as you go along.

Now you have a website to be proud of, so in the next chapter, we'll look at how to get noticed.

Activity: SEO training

Check out the SEO training and help for the platform your website is on and familiarise yourself with how to optimise your website and blog posts. If you're a technophobe, just take it slowly, it doesn't have to be perfect, and you can learn as you go along.

Your Growth Journal: Questions for reflection

- Complete the sentence: I do my best when...
- Reflect on a time when you struggled to master a piece of technology but mastered it. How did that feel? How did it benefit you?

CHAPTER 18 CONTENT MARKETING

First things first, what exactly IS content marketing? According to Wikipedia, content marketing is 'a form of marketing focused on creating, publishing, and distributing content for a targeted audience online. It is often used by businesses in order to:

- Attract attention and generate leads
- Expand their customer base
- Generate or increase online sales
- Increase brand awareness or credibility
- Engage an online community of users'

Content marketing is basically:

- Writing blogs
- Creating videos
- Producing audios/podcasts.
- Some aspects of social media

Content Marketing

The majority of therapists tend to use blogging as a way of producing and sharing content, so in this chapter, I shall be referring to creating content as blogging. However, it covers all content creation.

Producing content is a great way for any business to be more visible and attract clients using the oh so important know, like and trust factor, but for us as therapists, it's **perfect** for so many reasons because:

- You're connecting with people
- You're helping people freely and for free
- You're raising your visibility
- You attract clients without ever having to be 'salesy'.
- You can be creative
- You're letting your personal qualities/personality show, creating connection

As therapists, we have a huge amount of information that can be used to help people. Our biggest problem, in my experience, is self-belief.

In *'Friend, not foe: blogging for counsellors'*, Bethany Bray explores how professional counsellors don't have enough of a voice online:

'Conduct an Internet search for any mental health topic – i.e., suicidal behaviour in teenagers, group therapy for single moms, eating disorders among college students – and you'll find a wealth of blogs

The top hits that come up in your search, however, will likely be blogs written by social workers, educators or other helping professionals – not professional counsellors.'

Content Marketing

Counsellors and therapists as a profession are missing out on this amazing opportunity to both help people, attract clients and raise the profile of counselling. We are doing ourselves, our profession and the public a disservice by NOT producing and sharing content. If we want to give therapy a rebrand, we need to address this.

Let's take a look at some of the benefits:

Establish authority

When you produce content, you'll establish authority in your niche as it demonstrates your knowledge and skills in your specialist area and gives you the status of 'expert'. We discussed being an expert in earlier, so you know our tendency to be shy about our abilities can really hamper the therapeutic process.

From a business perspective, it's important to be seen as highly knowledgeable and skilled; otherwise potential clients will find someone that is. By producing content, you don't have to call yourself an expert, but you'll be seen as one.

Therapy Rebrand

As I said right at the start of this book, I think counselling needs a rebrand: many people are terrified of going to see a therapist. There's a perception of the therapist being someone in authority, a bit tweedy and 'holier than thou' - which as you'll know is (mostly) nonsense! I believe that as a profession, we need to collectively change that, and content marketing is a perfect way to connect with the public and allay those fears.

Think back to when you've had counselling, what did you look for when choosing a therapist? Qualifications and experience - yes, you need to feel that you're in safe hands, but you also need warmth from the therapist, you need to know they will understand you. After all, the therapeutic relationship is paramount in pretty much all modalities.

Producing content on '10 ways you can avoid a panic attack' or 'how to use mindfulness to reduce stress' doesn't cross any personal disclosure boundaries but does give the perfect opportunity to let your warmth come through and over time your personality will show. Then you'll have the know, like, and trust factor which will attract the right clients for you.

Inform and help

Regular and consistent blogging means you'll produce a valuable resource. Again, having a niche directs people to you as the expert, so if your speciality is issues around anger, for example, you can answer questions to peoples most commonly asked questions, like 'How to recognise your anger triggers' and 'How to express angry feelings safely'.

SEO

Google loves authority, and by producing content, we inform the search engines that we have something useful to say. SEO stands for Search Engine Optimisation, which is the process of letting search engines like Google know who you are and what you do so they will show you in the right searches. Check out chapter 17 for more about SEO.

Drive traffic

Posting a keyword rich blog regularly lets the search engines know you have interesting information to share, so they will rank your website higher. If you want to be on page one, get writing!

The same applies for podcasts and videos: you have an SEO optimised webpage for every episode you produce with the show notes, i.e. what this episode covered, any links to share, links to

Content Marketing

related content etc. Some people share a transcription of the show or an audio-only version of the video. Having such useful, informative content on your site means you can direct people over to your site to consume it. The more visitors, the more visible you get, the more search engines rank your website and the more you show up in searches. It's a virtuous circle, and the more visitors you get to your website, the more enquiries you'll receive and ultimately more clients.

Stand out

There are so many counsellors and trainee counsellors around that to make a living and attract your ideal client, you need to stand out from the crowd. Producing content about your niche elevates you among a sea of others and gives you that edge.

Imagine this: your ideal client is searching for a therapist using one of the many online directories or Google. They feel overwhelmed as there are so many therapists to choose from, so they pick three to check out. They land on your website, which is warm and speaks directly to them. They see that you write blogs, so go and take a look. The blogs all address issues and topics they are struggling with. They get a sense of you, that you understand their issues and can help, so you become the obvious choice.

Blogging and then sharing those blogs effectively via social media will grow your practice.

Get noticed

In my time, blogging has got me noticed in many ways:

- As a direct result of a blog I wrote, I was invited to talk at a BACP (British Association for Counsellors and Psychotherapists) conference

- I was been interviewed by Therapy Today (BACP monthly publication)
- I was interviewed on local radio several times
- I was interviewed many times online and on podcasts

It has opened doors for me, and it can open doors for you.

It's low cost or free

Advertising is expensive. Not only that, there's no guaranteed return on investment (ROI). You can get started producing content for your website by writing or simply using your phone to record audio or video. It will take some time, but one well-written blog post can work hard: you can promote that blog all over social media many times over and in lots of different ways for years to come.

It may be time consuming at first, but the more you do something, the quicker you get. To start with it will probably take ages, but as you get going and find a method and system that's right for you, it will get quicker and easier.

Imagine each blog post brings you one new client: how much money does that bring? For me, I average about 12 sessions per client or more. 12 x my fee is well worth the time it takes to write. I can't say how many clients a blog will attract for you, but it's definitely the gift that keeps on giving as each post can be recycled and repurposed many times over and used it lots of different ways.

When you write a blog, it's not about writing, sharing and then leaving it to gather dust in the recesses of your website. It's about getting every last drop of marketing juice out of every blog, and we do this by recycling and repurposing content.

Content Marketing

This is *genius* as it saves you so much time! You've already done the hard work by producing it, now you can use it again and again in different ways. I'll give you an example:

Imagine you've written a blog '7 ways to get a good night's sleep'. Here are some ways you can repurpose it:

- After it's published, do a quick 2-3-minute live broadcast on social media introducing the blog post and what readers get from it
- Share the post on social media, introducing it to spark curiosity, so people click through and read it

For **each of** the 7 tips:

- Write a short social media post
- Make the tip into an attractive image
- Copy, paste and tweak the whole tip to share as a long form social media post (which is like a mini blog post).
- Do a live broadcast
- Take quotes from your blog and share either as text or create some attractive images
- Create an infographic of the 7 tips
- Whenever there is something in the media about sleep, share your blog and direct them to the relevant part.
- Check for awareness days where you can share it further

That's a potential 44+ different ways you can use that single blog post to raise your profile and get seen, all with the added bonus of helping people, and there are many more ways to repurpose content. The best bit is, you can do this another 3 or 4 times a year. See - the gift that just keeps on giving!

We'll look more about sharing content in the chapter on social media.

There are two types of content: one is evergreen content that is always relevant and can be shared at any time. Then there is time specific content, so posts that refer to things like Christmas, Mother's Day, Valentine's day, etc., so they can only really be shared at these times. There's a place for both, and both can be recycled and repurposed to reuse them and take the maximum marketing juice from each, but it makes sense to not reference something that's very topical in a post which can date it quickly.

On my previous site (janetravis.com) which was about self-care for people pleasers, some of my blog posts have been shared thousands of times - one well over 100k times. That gets my work in front of a whole lot of people.

Producing content gives you something fantastic to share with your social media followers, produced especially to help your ideal clients with the issues they have providing visibility and connection.

And regular content production about your chosen niche encourages you to keep up to date and continue learning about your speciality.

Consistency

Producing content regularly is important, so decide on a schedule and stick with it whether that's weekly, fortnightly or monthly. I wouldn't recommend longer than a month between publishing pieces of content.

Prioritise your content production and have space and time to produce it regularly.

Batching is a very time effective way of producing content, especially for podcasts and videos. Basically, you plan and prepare your episodes in advance and then write or record them all in one sitting. If producing recorded content, depending on how long your episodes are, you can get many done - 3 months' worth or more.

Similarly, if you are blogging, you can concentrate on planning and writing blog posts over a week to produce several at a time - great for those quiet spells.

Batching is extremely time effective, as you can get into that creative headspace, get them written or recorded and you don't have to think about it again for a while.

Finding your voice

Finding your voice is an interesting concept because you already have one. You already have a style that's unique to you, so mostly 'finding your voice' is an exercise in having the confidence to write from the heart. Your writing style will be slightly different depending on who you are writing for. Having a niche will help you identify your style as writing for stressed executives will be different from writing for university students. But whoever you're writing for, have a conversational style. Blogging is casual, and you aren't expected to know the answer to life's issues, so don't put yourself under that pressure.

What can you talk about?

Content marketing is all about helping your ideal clients with whatever issues they have, so go back to The Empathy Exercise and look at their day - what would help them?

Content Marketing

Answering questions is always a great thing to do because it doesn't only help your clients, it's also great for your SEO (we cover this in the SEO chapter).

There is inspiration all around you if you think outside the box:

Overheard conversations

I was in the doctor's waiting room, and a young mother with her toddler was waiting too. The little girl was being well behaved and quiet, but every time she spoke, the mother would hush her. It made me think about the effect that might have on her, why the mother felt they had to silence their child, the pressures that parents have with young children to control them, fears of criticism etc and it made me wonder if here in the UK, we still believe that children should be seen but not heard. Interesting stuff which would make some interesting blogs.

Be aware of what's happening around you and consider how it can be made into a blog post.

Read books and blogs

Reading expands the mind, so read books and blogs, but not necessarily about counselling. Read blogs from other genres, like yoga, massage, organisation or productivity, and you'll be surprised how it can inspire you.

Storytelling

This is how I like my coffee: I like milk in first, ⅓ spoon of sugar and quite milky (skimmed milk). Previously I didn't ask for my coffee the way I liked it because of fears that I'd be thought of as fussy or awkward, so I was given coffee that, to me, tasted like dishwater that was far too sweet.

But one day I changed and started to ask if they would mind putting the milk in first please and make it quite milky with ⅓ spoon of sugar. I noticed that people didn't mind at all, and actually, it would be something we'd joke about. Most people, given the chance, will do things to make you happy, but we don't always give them a chance. How I like my coffee is widely known now, and it's become something that's quirky about me.

This story about coffee isn't earth-shattering, but it was a lesson about asking for our needs to be met, why we don't and how when we do, people are often okay with it. This story will be remembered because it's light-hearted and certainly not preachy. When people read it, they will identify their own issues around asking for what they want.

Can you see how aspects of the theory are playing out around you, like the drama triangle, defence mechanisms, self-sabotage? You don't have to name them as such, but you could explore them in a blog

What family stories have you broken through? Maybe you'd always believed you couldn't do something but discovered you could.

Are there any well know stories or fairy tales you can adapt? For example, in Frozen, for example, when Elsa's parents said her powers were bad and dangerous, that could that have been a form of emotional abuse. The well-meaning parents got it wrong and left her feeling like a bad person that couldn't live a normal life which went on to have a massive impact on her.

Don't overthink it. The coffee story came to mind as I stopped to grab a coffee while writing this section! Just be open to looking creatively at everyday situations.

Questions

What questions do your clients have? Questions like 'What happens in the first session of counselling?' would make a great blog as it helps to allay fears around coming to see you. Or 'how to' questions, like' How do I start making new friends after a bereavement?', or 'How do I say no without causing conflict'.

Blogging

What is a blog? A blog is a casually written communication with your reader. It's not an essay or a report, and it's not a place to use big words or confusing counselling terms. If an 11 year old doesn't understand it, change it. This isn't because we are being patronising to readers, but because consuming a blog should be easy. You're not being a teacher or a preacher, just are just inviting people to consider different ideas. As with everything, it's all about the client, so answer their common questions and reflect on their common issues.

Writing is a skill that you learn over time, and it's like a muscle: the more you do it, the stronger it becomes. Your writing will always improve over time. When I look back at my early blogs, they make me smile and appreciate how far my writing has come - I mean, look, I'm writing a book!

Audio/Podcasts

If you don't like the thought of writing, podcasts could be a great choice for you. Podcasts have been growing enormously over the last few years, and now there are thousands on all sorts of subjects. I listen to a lot as they are so easy to consume. I can listen when walking the dog, doing housework or driving so I am learning new things all the time as well as being entertained.

Content Marketing

I highly recommend the Minimum Viable Product (MVP) approach to getting started, which means just get out there using what you have and try it out before investing a lot of money into equipment. You can record audio on your mobile phone, which is fine when starting out though you will want to get a better quality microphone if you decide to continue. Often podcasts come in 'seasons' so you could record 6, 10, 12 all in one go, publish them weekly and see how it goes.

Commit to doing twelve and use it as an experiment to see how you enjoy it and give yourself full permission to stop after the twelve you have committed to. Put everything into it and see how it goes. Worst case scenario, you delete the lot. Best case scenario, you have a fantastic, free way to connect with potential clients and become the go-to expert. All your recordings can be repurposed and recycled.

There are many formats you could try, but the most popular seem to be each week talking about a different topic or interviewing a guest, though you can mix and match. Your podcast, your rules. Subjects to talk about would be the same as blog posts, and you can use The Empathy Exercise from chapter 15 to explore listeners pain points and ideal outcomes.

Video/YouTube

People are often absolutely terrified of video! In my experience, there comes a point when someone somewhere encourages you enough for you to run out of excuses, so you give it a try. You make your first, nervous and shaky Facebook live broadcast and realise that actually, that was okay. Not only okay, but they enjoyed it! It's a little like the first karaoke you go to, where you vow you'll never sing, but after getting up with your friends and blasting out 'I will survive', they have to wrestle the mic from your hands!

Start with the MVP, which can simply be recording using your mobile phone, and as before commit to doing twelve as an experiment will full permission to not carry on if you discover it's not for you.

Which is the right one for you?

All these methods of producing content are effective, so it's down to you which you prefer. Producing content is something you'll be doing regularly and consistently, so by doing things you enjoy, you'll make the whole process easier for yourself. Whichever you choose, there will be a learning curve to navigate, but all of these can be learned over time.

Your website is really starting to take shape now: you have your niche, you're speaking directly to your clients, your branding and your content. In the next chapter, we look at how can you get more people to visit your site.

Activity: Brainstorm

10 minute brainstorm. Grab the work you did with The Empathy Exercise, and brainstorm 20 questions your ideal clients would ask. Then type them in Google to see if anyone is looking for those things - it's quite an eye-opener!

Your Growth Journal: Questions for reflection

- Which appeals to you: blogging, producing videos or podcasting, and why?
- If you have a little voice in your head saying you can't do it, who's voice is that? What would you like to say to them?

CHAPTER 19 SOCIAL MEDIA

Social media is another one of those fantastic tools we have available to us for free. I started in practice at roughly the same time as Facebook started, so I can remember what life was like before social media became what it is today and I can tell you, running a practice was a whole lot more expensive. We had the limited choice of advertising in local newspapers (remember them?) which were pricey, and you had no say in where that advert would appear. Your ad could be hidden away in the back of the publication on a page no one saw. Or you could advertise in the Yellow Pages. There has always been a free entry you can have which is just your name and phone number, but to stand out you needed a boxed advert which was also expensive, and you had to deal with extremely pushy salespeople.

Now we have social media, and you can connect with hundreds, thousands, even millions of people for free and is very effective if used well.

Social Media

Social media changes quickly. For example, a while ago, I put together some training on Facebook pages. I prepared slides and did a quick run through in preparation to record the following day. The next day I started recording the training, clicking through on my Facebook demo page as planned, but it had all changed overnight. I had to rewrite and re-record the whole darned thing.

For this reason, I won't be looking at specific tips and techniques on what to post in this book. However, there are some general principles that are unlikely to go out of date, and I'll share those here.

One of the issues with social media is it can become a massive time suck. I often see people spending far too long fiddling with social media and doing 'busy' work - things that make you feel like you're working, but actually, you're spending a long time doing something that either doesn't really matter or doesn't achieve much.

Social media is literally designed to keep you there as long as possible, with notifications and alerts that encourage you to just keep on scrolling. It's so important to manage the time spent there, or you can waste hours.

Another issue is being consistent, otherwise, you may find that you haven't posted on social media for a few days/weeks, and then panic and post something - anything - just to get something out there. It's okay, it happens, but posting in this haphazard way isn't going to bring you the results you want, because what you post isn't likely to be high quality. Organisation is key. Let's look at some pain-free ways to do that:

- Keep it simple

- Choose just one platform
- Check-in twice a day

Hold on, did she just say one platform? Yes, she did!

Choose one social media platform

We've looked at how important it is to get focussed on what you're doing. When you have direction, you get more done in less time. Without focus, the pull to procrastination is strong.

People are often on more than one social media platform because of FOMO - Fear Of Missing Out, believing that they'll be more visible if they are on all the platforms. Maybe they worry that if other therapists are on other platforms, they will take all the clients - remember when we talked about a 'lack' mindset? But each platform has **millions** of users, so growing your audience, increasing engagement and connecting fully on one platform will bring far better results than a half-hearted presence on several. Use your time - and energy - wisely.

It may not feel like it takes much time to copy posts over to other platforms, but you can't engage fully on all of them, and on many platforms, you are rewarded for engagement, which we'll cover this later. It has an impact on you energetically as you have to reply to comments, accept follower requests and then feel the pressure to work more fully on that platform. This just waters down your social media message, and it takes up more of your valuable time. It's going to leave you feeling frustrated that your social media efforts aren't bringing results, which can lead to those negative mindset issues like telling yourself you can't do this, which is rubbish as you totally can.

Using just one platform means you'll learn how to use all the functions that the platform has to the best of your abilities and learn all the best practices, making it far more effective.

One platform means you can concentrate all your efforts on growing a following in one place.

Your love affair with social media

Let's imagine you're going to start a relationship with social media. First, you have to decide which one you are most attracted to. They are all different:

- LinkedIn is a great way to connect both locally and globally and is easy to grow your connections
- Twitter is fast-moving and chatty
- Instagram is visual and creative
- Facebook is multi-faceted, with personal profiles, pages, groups and many users. But it's strict, you have to play by the rules to be successful - and the rules change often

I'm not including Pinterest here as it's not a social media platform, it's a search engine, and it's really not a good choice for people wanting to attract people in the local area. However, if you are an online therapist, this could be a great choice for sharing the content you produce.

Each social media platform has rules, things they encourage you to do and things you will be penalised for. These are called algorithms which are a set of rules used to decide what content is seen. Long gone are the days of a chronological feed, today you get what you're given. This can be really annoying when not all your followers get to see what you post, but for what social media gives us it's worth playing by the rules so you can get your message in front of a large number of people.

Which platform do you fancy?

Name

It's rare that your name or practice name will be available on social media now as so many millions of people use social media it's probably been taken. You have to get creative about what handle you choose. But first, let's look at what makes a good social media name.

It should be short: on Twitter, your username is no longer than 15 characters (a character is a-z, 1-0 and underscores). Using numbers and underscores isn't ideal and should be avoided if possible, but sometimes it's just not possible. You can also use some sort of abbreviation of your name. For example, my practice name is Reflections Counselling Lincoln, and I chose ReflectionsOn_ The most important thing is to make it easy to remember and for you to say, '*come follow me on [platform], I'm XXX*'.

Although I recommend only concentrating on one platform, go and claim that name across all platforms. There are websites to help you with this, where you type in the name, and it will check all platforms and also come up with a few alternative ideas.

The bottom line is if you can't get the perfect name, it's no big deal. Most often, people find your social media by clicking on a link, and they don't even register what that name was. If you can get your desired name that's brilliant, but don't lose sleep over it.

Bio

Your social media bio will change depending on the platform you are on. Twitter only gives you a very limited number of words you can use, whereas LinkedIn gives you room for a lot of information. Think carefully about what you want on your bio, use keywords where you can and use the Niche Statement and The Empathy Exercise to help you write it.

First dates

Now is the exciting time in the relationship where you really start to get to know each other. Familiarise yourself with your chosen platform and find out what it does, what it likes, and what annoys it. As in a real relationship situation, this changes regularly, so part of your job as a business owner is to keep up to date with changes on your social media platform and tweak your social media strategy accordingly. You can do this by following experts in your chosen platform or joining us in the Grow Your Private Practice Club.

When the honeymoon period is over

There comes a point in every relationship when that exciting period ends and things settle into a routine. This is where the cracks start to show, and you see your differences more clearly, or you start to feel neglected, working hard and getting nothing back. As with all relationships, this is when you have to put in the work.

It's easy to point the finger of blame in relationships and blame the platform for not being good enough, not working, not bringing you results, and it's easy to have your head turned by a newer, sexier platform. But if you want a quality relationship with your social media (and not keep going from one unfulfilling relationship to another), now is the time to get honest with yourself.

Before you think 'Pah! LinkedIn is rubbish!' and go have an affair with Twitter, take a good look at your part in this, and ask yourself, do I know how to:

- Get more attention
- Attract interest
- Increase engagement
- Connect with other local people/businesses
- Use all the functions,
- Grow my followers
- Use analytics to find the best times to post
- Use analytics to see which posts are most popular

What has your part in this unfulfilling relationship been? Have you been neglecting it? Have you taken it for granted? Have you expected it to do all the work for you? Did you get a bit lazy? Show it some love, and you'll soon feel fulfilled again.

Engagement

Engagement is a huge part of your social media success. This is SOCIAL media, people are on there because they want to be social, so post fun, interesting things that encourage people to interact. Please don't just use social media as a way to advertise yourself, i.e. 'Therapist in London, slots available now, call me' as people just don't react well to being sold to. You'll really miss out on the amazing potential social media can bring. Social media is so much more than that.

What do I mean by engagement? Well, social media platforms want to keep people on their sites as that's how they get their advertising revenue. If people click away via a link in your post that encourages people to leave, which isn't good for them, or if people don't seem to take an interest in what you have to say and never like, comment or share your posts, your posts will be considered dull and won't be shown to many.

Consequently, they operate algorithms which dictate how many people will be shown what you post.

If you share something with a link that takes people away from the platform, it simply won't show people what you've written because it knows that post is encouraging people to click away.

However, if you produce social media posts that people engage in, i.e., they like the post, leave a comment or share it, then it will be deemed to be a good, interesting or entertaining post which encourages people to stay on their platform. You are rewarded for these posts by more of your future posts being shown to your followers. Therefore, the more posts you can make that get this engagement, the more people will get to see what you post and the more successful your social media campaign.

No engagement = no one sees your posts.

Lots of engagement = more people see what you post.

And I think we can agree that if we are going to take the time, trouble and effort to use social media, we want it to be as successful as possible.

The best way to make the most of your social media is to plan in advance what you're going to say. We talked about time blocking in chapter 11, and now you'll see why I recommend it.

In my monthly planning meetings in the Grow Your Private Practice Club, we follow a formula, which I'll share with you as an example.

You can use content that you have produced this month to dictate your social media themes. If you've written a blog post on '7 ways to get a good night's sleep', you can use that post to

Social Media

dictate what you share over at least a week. Day 1, introduce the blog and let people know what problem you are solving, then you can share something from each of the 7 ways.

For example:

- Share a quote (with or without an image) but explain why you particularly like this quote. Just a quote image on its own no longer gets noticed
- Go live on social media and talk for a few minutes about sleep
- Ask a simple question about sleep, like 'what time do you go to bed at night', which is very easy for people to respond to
- Ask an either/or question like 'do you sleep with windows open or windows closed?'.

See how you can use just very simple questions that are easy for people to answer? This will really increase your engagement.

If you haven't produced any content this week, you can either re-purpose an older blog post or choose a theme for the week.

Social media weekly themes

Here are some themes counsellors can use that cover all niches:

- Relaxation
- Being social
- Creativity
- Time alone
- Letting go of responsibility
- Eating
- Drinking

- Money
- Relationships
- Sex
- Needs
- Planning
- Organisation
- Personal care/appearance
- Friendship
- Sleep
- Exercise
- Meditation
- Mindfulness
- Hobbies
- Music
- Decluttering

Then use the CAR method:

- C=Connection
- A=Authority
- R=Real person

C = Connection post

This is the kind of content that gets your audience to talk back to you, so ask easy to answer questions like 'this or that' (do you prefer the cinema or Netflix). It's just about connection, so it doesn't necessarily have to be counselling related. Take a moment to notice how questions like this are simple to answer.

If people take the time to comment, make sure you always respond to each and every person. Always 'like' the comment and reply if appropriate. After all, if you take the time to write a comment and you get acknowledged, how do you feel?

If your weekly theme is friendship, some connection post ideas could be:

- Question: How often do you get together with friends?
- This or that: Do you prefer to chat on the phone or go for coffee?
- Poll: What's your favourite way to spend time with friends: Coffee, lunch, pub, cook a meal, do an activity?
- What's missing? Write a short list of things and ask what's missing. For example, 'Things I look for in a friend': Acceptance, humour, good listener, supportive, ... What would you add?

Can you see how simple these are to answer? People love to have their say, to join in the conversation and share their opinions, so relax and have some fun with it.

A = Authority post

These posts highlight your expertise but not in a showy way, in a way that feels comfortable to you.

Some authority post ideas are:

- A book recommendation and why you recommend it
- Apps you recommend and why
- A testimonial (if you collect them)
- Answer a common question (great for a live broadcast)
- Share a quote (with or without image) and why you like this particular quote

It's sharing the reason *why* you recommend or like something that makes you the authority.

R = Real person

Here you share small snippets of yourself which makes you relatable, approachable and human. Remember, many people accessing therapy are terrified, so these small snippets of you as a human helps people to connect with you and allay fears.

An example could be sharing simple photos, like your afternoon coffee and cake, something about your pet, thoughts on a film or a story about something you've overcome.

Therapy Rebrand

In the introduction to this book, I talked about the Therapy Rebrand survey I did and highlighted the need for us to get comfortable with social media. If you recall, people expressed anxiety around talking to a stranger or finding the right therapist. Well, connection and real person posts are your ideal opportunity to allow people to see your warmth and personality come through. It stops you from being a stranger.

Be sure you are providing value to readers. Answer common questions, give tips, offer thoughts for reflection and be entertaining. Allow your true voice to be heard: if you're a light-hearted person, let that shine, if you are more of a deep thinker, let that reflective sideshow. It's all about connection, so trust that the right people will connect with you. For example, my posts tend to be light-hearted and fun which attracts clients who like that, but it will drive some people mad - which is fine, they will connect with the right person for them.

Consistency

Planning and scheduling will bring you that oh so important consistency, which really is vital and the trust part of the know, like and trust trilogy. Compare this with realising you haven't posted anything for 3 weeks, panic and just post anything and you can see how the results will be far better.

Put aside time in your month to devote to just planning your social media, and once you have it planned, you can get things scheduled to post to your platform automatically, which will be a godsend. There are many ways you can schedule your posts either directly onto the platform or by using an app, some of which are free. This means you can schedule them to be posted automatically on the day and time you want. Schedule out as much as you can, then you can get all your social media done in one go in a short space of time.

Because you're focusing on your social media strategy in one sitting, you will be in a more creative headspace and your social media efforts will be more effective. You can plan and schedule a month's social media in an hour, though it will take longer when just starting out so allow for this, and don't expect miracles. Obviously, if you have planned a live broadcast, you can't do that in advance, but you can prepare what you are going to say, note your bullet points and promote it so more people watch.

It's not all about posting

We've taken a good look at what to post on social media, but it's not all about posting, it's also about forming relationships and networking. Part of your time should be spent connecting with other people, businesses and charities in your local area. Like their posts and make comments that add to the conversation. This helps you be visible.

This doesn't have to take much time. Go into your social media twice a day for just 10 minutes and use a timer for this or you'll get distracted. 'Like' ALL comments you get and respond to comments wherever possible. Then connect with other users to grow your connections. Know what you're going to do, go in, do it and come out again. Stay focussed, and don't fall down that social media rabbit hole.

What training do I need?

No matter how comfortable you are using your chosen platform, it's always good to keep learning and improving, so follow experts, read their blogs, listen to their podcasts and watch some training on YouTube. Keep abreast of new developments and pick up new ideas to try. Have curiosity and an open mind.

In the Grow Your Private Practice Club, we look at social media and content in our monthly planning meetings, so join us for ideas and inspiration.

Can I ever have more than one platform?

If you are using your social media platform to its best, planning and scheduling your social media and engaging with and increasing your followers, you won't really need a second one. But if you choose to start on another, always keep your main platform as your number one, and focus most of your attention there.

As with any relationship, the more you focus on it and prioritise its needs, the more you get from it. Love your social media, and it will love you back.

With things like social media and content creation being (mostly) free and extremely effective, is there still a need to advertise our practice in the traditional sense? We take a look at this in the next chapter.

Activity: Choose your social media account

If you've been in practice a while it's possible you have more than one social media account, so decide which you want to focus on and write a short post on the others directing them to your main platform.

Then give your account a facelift using information from The Empathy Exercise.

Your Growth Journal: Questions for reflection

- What sort of personality do you have, and how can you express this in your social media?
- How do you feel about using social media? What fears come up for you?

CHAPTER 20 ADVERTISING AND OFFLINE MARKETING

The online world has opened up a new world of marketing possibilities that just ten years ago, we could only dream about.

- You can produce and broadcast a video for free to hundreds/thousands/millions of people
- You can connect with people from the comfort of your own home
- You can get your message out to exactly who you want to and target your ideal clients

However, as wonderful as the online marketing possibilities are, nothing will replace face to face conversations and the real-life connections of actually getting out there and talking to people. You are far more likely to be remembered, and if you're remembered, you'll get referrals.

Advertising And Offline Marketing

It's also a great way of combating isolation because you are connecting with people and forming business relationships and friendships. It's inexpensive and will get you known quickly.

Offline marketing is also brilliant if you are just starting out as a counsellor, which is why networking is included in the Quickstart section.

Networking

One of the best ways to get known in your local area and start making connections is through business networking, and I highly recommend it. I've spoken about this at length in chapter 6, so to learn about the benefits and the practicalities head on over there.

Advertising?

I'm often asked what is the best place to advertise, and it's not a simple one size fits all answer.

There are considerations, like what's your niche? What skills do you have? How many clients are you looking to attract? How much money do you have to invest? What have you already done?

As a counsellor running a private practice, paid advertising isn't usually the best investment for your business because your advert has to get in front of exactly the right person at exactly the right time if you're going to attract them as clients.

Consider how people access counselling: they recognize they need some extra help and do one or both of these things:

Talk to a friend, and the friend recommends someone they have used themselves or know of

OR

Research local therapists via Google

Generally, people don't flick through a magazine, stumble across an advert about therapy and think *'Ooh, that's what I need.'*. Which means that advertising is a gamble. You have the odds stacked against you. You need the stars aligned so that your ad is seen by the right person at exactly the time they are ready to access help.

I treat paid advertising like I do lending money to friends; I only do it if I can afford to not get the money back. If I either pay to advertise or lend money, it's only ever relatively small amounts. I can't afford to lose £500.

If you have the money to invest in your practice, it may be a risk worth taking. Experiment with it and see what types of advertising works. But as with gambling, don't spend what you can't afford to lose.

However, there are some places to consider targeted advertising that can be a good choice for therapists.

Directories

One of the main ways for counsellors to advertise is in online directories. When I started out, they worked very well, but now that there are so many counsellors around it can be hit and miss. Check out chapter 4 for more about directories

Local magazines

Local 'parish magazine' type publications can be good. People often keep hold of copies and refer to them when they want a local service. If they see your ad in there, they might remember it to use themselves or share with someone that needs it. But don't pay a lot because in my experience they can be hit and miss. Again, have a trial period and monitor the results.

Facebook Ads

Facebook ads can be a very cost-effective way to advertise as you can directly target your ideal clients. However, if you're going to use them, be sure to get some training, or it's an easy way to lose money. You'll find loads of information on using Facebook Ads, so do your homework first to get the most from it. Again, this is something that changes regularly, so be sure to keep up to date with best practices.

Google Ads

Lots of therapists have had success with Google Ads, though as with Facebook Ads, you need to do your homework to get the most out of it. Payment is on a Pay Per Click (PPC) basis, so you only pay when people click through to your website. Google Ads changes frequently, so again I'm not going to look at any specifics here.

Pay for advertising sparingly and monitor what advertising works for you by asking new clients how they found you.

IMPORTANT: Be wary of people that contact you to sell advertising space. Is what they are offering something you have been planning to do? There are scams out there, so tell them you will get back to them and do your homework. Genuine companies will be fine with this. Never buy because you feel pressured. Stay safe.

Leaflets

Leaflets can be a cost-effective but time-consuming way of getting your name out. Leaflets are basically your advertisement, and you can share them pretty much anywhere that will accept them.

Advertising And Offline Marketing

However, something that I find more useful is producing a help sheet or checklist that your ideal clients would find useful that you can give away. People like free gifts, and if they find it useful, you will be remembered. It's also far less salesy because it's simply about helping people, but it will have your branding and contact details on.

For example, if you work with children, producing a help sheet for parents to stay sane in the summer holidays or Christmas would be very useful. Then you can approach a school, and instead of asking to advertise via them, you'd be saying 'I have these free help sheets, do you think they would help your parents/kids?' That's going to make a yes far more likely than 'can I advertise to your parents?'

Business cards

Before you get business cards printed, think about how you will use them. I confess I have spent hours faffing around with business cards only to end up with hundreds gathering dust in a drawer. I don't want that to happen to you.

If you plan to do a lot of networking, you will need some, though when you start out some basic ones will do fine. Otherwise, you can get away with not having any.

If you do have some, here are some ways you can use them:

- Keep a bag in your car that contains posters, leaflets, business cards, Sellotape and drawing pins. Then anytime you see a place you can put a poster, leaflet or card you have everything there and ready
- Always keep cards in your bag, you never know when you'll need them

Advertising And Offline Marketing

- Take them to any networking or training event where you meet new people. When you exchange cards, always follow up with an 'it was so nice to meet you' email, so they remember you, and you start a relationship. Remember, this is about building relationships not selling your services - so what can you do to help them? Connect on social media too. Do this and not only will you grow your networking circle and build business friendships and relationships, but you'll also get more referrals. We play the long game, consistency is key
- Leave them almost anywhere with permission - supermarkets, doctors, funeral directors etc. Some places give permission, and some don't. I have found that it's usually the smaller ones that do, but it's always worth asking
- Give a client one at their first appointment, then any changes or planned annual leave times are written on the back of another one and given again for every change
- Give one at the end of therapy
- Put them up on Community Centre noticeboards
- Deliver one to all the houses in walking distance from yours/your practice.
- Enlist family and friends to help and ask them to display leaflets on the staff notice board, leave cards in the staff room or on the front desk at work

Workshops

Workshops can be free or paid, but let's take a look at free. When I first started as a counsellor, I offered free workshops, and it's a fantastic way of standing out and showcasing your expertise and knowledge.

Think of something that fits with your niche but is also pretty general, and for inspiration, check the list of topics in chapter 18.

Consider of the time of year: Christmas survival guide, the single girls guide to having a great Valentine's day. Maybe there is a national event you could be part of, or something general, like stress reduction or how to say no. Then approach places where you think this would be of use. If you already have somewhere in mind, approach them with maybe two or three suggestions, and then write the one they want.

You can have whatever format or style you want. I'd consider a formal workshop to be where I'm standing in front of people, maybe with a PowerPoint presentation. With this, you need to prepare and practice. Or you could offer to come in on a casual basis with some information and just be available to chat. Try approaching mother and toddler groups, workplaces (maybe lunchtime in the canteen) libraries, health centres, gyms and youth clubs.

Looking outside the box

Here are some things to try that are a little outside the box:

- Collaborate with a cafe, undertaker, vet, gym, hairdresser etc
- Consider national charity events - Macmillan coffee morning, Red Nose Day etc
- School fetes: book a table - often free - and have help sheets to give out. Talk to people and make connections. Have some really simple things to do, like just get them to take 5 deep breaths with you. Possibly have a raffle to

Advertising And Offline Marketing

raise money for a charity to do with your niche, with raffle prizes that fit, e.g. a self-care pamper basket. Go with a colleague and make it a fun day out
- Public speaking: deliver a talk for the local Women's Institute meeting, or a youth club
- Radio guest: keep an eye out for what's happening in the news and approach the radio station with something topical you can help people with.

You are a counsellor in the counselling room, but outside the counselling room, you have valuable knowledge and skills you can share, which can help people, form local connections and gets you remembered. Check chapter 21 to see where could take you.

When you're out and about in your local area, be aware of what's around you. What events are happening that you could attend? What shops, organisations and other businesses are there you could work with? What charitable events are happening?

If you go to business networking groups, you can ask around, and find people to collaborate with, e.g. local massage therapists, hypnotherapists, chiropractors, acupuncturists could get together to host a wellness event.

There is no one size fits all for marketing your practice, so I'd like to encourage you to look outside the box, be creative and have fun.

How do all these marketing pieces fit together out there in the real world to get potential clients to contact you for an appointment? In the next chapter, we take a look at the client's journey into therapy.

Activity: Research local events

Research what events are happening in your local area and brainstorm ideas for how you can get involved.

Your Growth Journal: Questions for reflection

- What comes up for you when you think of in-person marketing?
- What one thing can you commit to trying?

CHAPTER 21 YOUR CLIENTS JOURNEY INTO THERAPY

As a private practitioner, it's useful to have an understanding of a clients journey into therapy. What are their thoughts, feelings and actions? What are the things that might put them off counselling as the choice they want to make?

We're going to look at four case studies depicting their journey into therapy.

1. Jenny

Jenny knows something is wrong but isn't exactly sure what.

Jenny has all the trappings of a nice house, job, family etc. and thought this would make her happy, but she just feels disappointed and unsatisfied. She can't sleep, feels anxious and has a low mood but has no idea why, so on top of her low mood she feels guilty and hasn't linked the dissatisfaction in her life to anxiety.

Would Jenny access therapy? Possibly not, because she hasn't yet identified what's happening for her. All she knows is she feels unhappy and doesn't really know why. Also, Jenny has prioritised the needs of other people above her own for all of her life, so the thought of spending time and money on herself doesn't sit well with her.

She doesn't see herself as having a mental health issue.

How you can reach people like Jenny?

Produce content and social media updates about raising self-esteem, improving self-care and noticing signs you might need help, like changes in normal patterns of eating, sleeping, etc. Highlight that counselling is a preventative measure, the best self-care you can get and that getting help early means it may not get worse. Also, talk about how the people around Jenny would also benefit if she was feeling better.

Normalise emotions like anger, jealousy, fear etc. with examples of how people react in certain circumstances to spark recognition.

Use Connection posts on social media. An example of a social media post could be:

'Sometimes it can be noble to put other people's needs before our own, but if we only do that we end up getting burnt out which isn't good for anyone - your kids, your partner, your job, your family, your friends, and most definitely not for you.

If you want to carry on being there for others, take some time out for yourself. Talk to a counsellor. You can share whatever you need to, and you will never be a burden. It's the ultimate self-care for both you and your family'.

This way, Jenny can start to connect with you as you're being helpful, and will start to see that she doesn't have to keep feeling this way. Should she decide to invest in counselling, you'll be top of mind.

2. Mark

Mark knows what's wrong but doesn't know there's a solution.

Mark is unhappy in his job. His boss takes advantage of his good nature, and he's expected to work ever longer hours, but he doesn't feel able to say anything.

It's not just his job. He often finds his friends and partners take advantage of him and mess him around. He flits between feeling angry and guilty, and then embarrassed, telling himself it's his fault for not being stronger and standing up for himself. He thinks he just has to put up with the situation, or there will be a conflict or some unpleasant outcome.

He's tried talking to friends, but they just tell him to say no to people, leaving him feeling that they don't understand his struggles.

He doesn't see himself as having a mental health issue.

How you can reach people like Mark?

Produce content and social media updates on self-care, communication and boundaries, and you can add in blogs that are 'case studies' - not real clients but made up ones. A great way to do this is to use characters from TV/films/books etc. to highlight a situation. For example, in '27 Dresses', the hero character had agreed to be a bridesmaid at two weddings at the same time and day because she didn't want to let down either of her friends, so she kept dashing from one wedding to the other,

Your Client's Journey Into Therapy

getting changed and changed back again. You could write about how she could have managed that situation without conflict or feeling guilty.

Or post something like this:

'We all know it's good to talk to people about our worries or issues, but have you ever noticed that they tend to not actually listen!? Sometimes they listen a while, and then talk about themselves, or that they've been through similar (or worse, which makes you feel bad!), or they offer unsolicited advice or plain tell you what to do. Or they try to trivialise your issues saying, 'Oh everyone feels like that'.

That's really unhelpful and makes us LESS likely to open up again - which is why we bottle things up in the first place.

Counsellors don't do that. We listen. I mean, really listen in order to understand and to help you work through some of your stuff. Have you ever been really listened to before? It's like being wrapped in a warm, comfy blanket. We are interested in you, your story and helping you to feel better. Try it! '

This way, Mark can start to connect with you as you are being helpful, and knows you understand that it's hard to 'just say no'. If he decides to invest in counselling, you'll be top of mind.

3. Felicity

Felicity knows there's a solution to her problem, but don't know which is right for her

Felicity is aware that she is struggling with the death of her mum three years ago, but she is unsure of the best way to help herself manage the situation. She has considered hypnotherapy, taking a holiday, enrolling in a self-help course and life coaching.

Your Client's Journey Into Therapy

She thinks therapy is for people with mental health issues, and she doesn't identify with that as she knows grief is a normal, natural reaction.

Which is why we, as therapists, need to keep talking and normalising what we do. Let people know that what they are experiencing is a normal response to their experiences and let them know that if they access therapy early, it may never develop into a mental health issue. That counselling is just the best self-care you can give yourself.

How you can reach people like Felicity?

As before, produce content and social media updates. Some ideas for content could be:

'I'm not depressed, do I need counselling?'

What can I hope to gain through counselling?

Manage your grief

Many people feel an element of guilt after someone has died as they remember every bad thought, every argument, every disappointment. You could post something like:

'Losing a loved one can be a confusing time. The grief and sadness can be peppered with angry thoughts, guilt over remembered arguments, unresolved issues and words that were left unsaid. Maybe you didn't get on with them, and you grieve the relationship that can now never be.

It can be hard to share such personal things with people, and we worry they won't understand or think we are unkind. But counsellors are there to listen, fully listen and we understand that relationships are complex. We can help lighten the load so you can make sense of that confusion and carry on with your life. And we are incredibly good at keeping secrets!

Ensure that your website offers Felicity hope. Consider what positive outcomes she might want? E.g. She might want to manage the intense anger she is still feeling at her mum being taken away so early.

Show her that therapy offers a solution, and if you feel unsure about 'promising' results, check out chapter 14 on messaging.

4. Ruth

Ruth knows they want therapy, but don't know if you're the right therapist for them.

Ruth knows she wants to access therapy to deal with childhood issues that are affecting her life but has no idea who to go to. She starts to Google local counsellors and is confused by the amount out there, all seemingly offering the same thing.

Then she lands on your website, which seems to really speak to her. She sees that you write blogs so goes to read a few, which are really helpful, and she likes your style. She sees your friendly face smiling back at her and can see a picture of the room you work from and can picture herself there. The FAQ page answers all her questions about fee's, parking etc. She can imagine herself talking with you and being understood. Then picks up the phone to call you.

All the work you have previously done with networking, producing content, social media etc. will demonstrate the know, like and trust factor and help her to connect with you.

You can see how all your marketing efforts will help you connect with potential clients at the different stages of their

Your Client's Journey Into Therapy

journey and different circumstances. This increases the likelihood of them choosing you for help above any other solutions out there.

So, what now? Well, the world is your oyster! There are many things you can do with the set of skills you have. In the next chapter, we do a little dreaming.

Activity: Brainstorm blocks

Consider your niche: Set your timer to 10 minutes, and brainstorm what are likely to be the blocks your ideal clients have about coming to counselling.

Your Growth Journal: Questions for reflection

- What would make someone choose you to work with and what words would attract them?
- Consider your own journey to personal therapy. What would have helped you make the choice to attend counselling earlier?

CHAPTER 22 TURNING YOUR DREAMS INTO GOALS

Becoming a therapist isn't something people just fall into, like the civil service. No, we choose to be a therapist, it's a calling. We feel passionate about helping people, about alleviating pain, about creating change and transformation.

Take yourself back to when you first started training as a therapist. Can you remember what drove you to embark on the expensive, time consuming and difficult training that's involved in becoming a counsellor? What was it that lit that fire under you?

Do you allow yourself to dream?

As a child, I used to dream about all sorts of things. I used to sit on the bus on the way home from school and dream about what it would be like to have a pony and be able to ride it every night. I'd dream about what I'd call it, what it would look like and the adventures we'd have, and it became so real I'd even be able to

Turning Your Dreams Into Goals

smell the leather of the tack.

But there was no way I could get a pony as a child. I had no money (obviously!), my parents couldn't afford it, and even if they could, I still couldn't because I'm very allergic to horses. But I'm not that little girl anymore!

As an adult, I can make that dream a reality, and if I choose to have a horse, I can. I can turn the dream into a goal and take steps to make it happen. I'd have to do my homework and work out how much it would cost, where to keep it, what was involved and whether I was prepared to take on the commitment, but I have a choice and can make it happen.

As adults, we tend to not dream as much. It can seem a bit childish, silly and a waste of time. Surely, we should just be more realistic and lower our expectations? After all, it saves on disappointment.

But here's the thing: recently, I *have* been allowing myself to dream again. I've been imagining what life would be like if I was successful, if I had more money, if I worked fewer hours and if I only did the things that I enjoyed, only making the choices that made me happy.

Guess what? I'm now able to see the possibility. I can actually make it happen, and as a result of this belief, my business has grown, but not only that, I have better work/life boundaries. If a client wants to see me at 7.30 pm on a Thursday, I now say 'I'm not available then but can do...' - and yes, I feel happier and more in control.

Dreaming has helped me to picture what I really want in my life and how I want to live it, which transformed into me taking steps to make that happen. It's given me a vision of how I would like my life to be.

Dreaming can be powerful - who knew? Well not me, but I'm seeing first-hand how dreaming is the first step towards having the life you want.

A dream is that part of you that thinks 'one day, I'll...'. What if that day was today?

What is a vision?

'A vision is a dream with a plan' Verne Harnish

A vision is a statement of where you want to be at some point in the future. It is born from your dreams and is connected to your values, passion and purpose. A vision is a plan for the future, it's something you want to become real. And without a plan, a dream just remains a dream, something that makes you sigh and think 'If only'.

Start with a dream, which becomes the vision, and from that, you can make goals which become actionable. Your goals enable you to take the steps needed to get you to your destination.

Possibilities

The beauty of being a counsellor is you can take your business into many different directions based upon your dreams, visions and goals. Traditionally therapy is two people sitting in a room together, but there are many other possibilities. You could offer online therapy, perfect if you don't have access to a room or like to travel. You could offer walk and talk therapy, out in nature. You can provide equine therapy and work with horses, group therapy and use a one to many business model.

You could run a training establishment, start a charity, be an activist for change, run retreats or write books. All of these things are possible.

But if you don't know where you're going, you'll not only get lost, you won't know when you've arrived at your destination.

As a therapist in private practice, you can work the hours that are convenient for you. If you have young kids, you may only want a few clients. Or you may only ever want to work part-time - being a therapist is hard, intense work, and I've only ever seen clients part-time and had other income sources around it. Or you may want to produce a full-time income from your therapy work. The choice is yours, and you can make it happen if you know what you want.

Goals

For some people, the thought of having goals can feel like pressure. What if I fail?

Goals are where we actually start taking action to make those dreams happen. It could be a client goal, where you want a certain number of clients, an income goal, or that you want to run a therapy retreat. It could be that you want to travel, so you offer online therapy.

This is why dreams are so important because when you're dreaming, you're purely exploring possibilities, trying on different options to see what fits. You're not looking at whether it's practical or how to do it.

You want to run a retreat? Well, it doesn't matter that you don't have the first clue how to do it, it only matters that you recognise you want to because when you know what you want to do, you can start figuring out how to make it happen. Work

Turning Your Dreams Into Goals

backwards from the outcome and work out what needs to be done to make it happen.

You can start doing some research, consider if you need any training or if you need a partner on board. Would you like your retreats to be in your home country or another country? Should they be luxury, high end, or priced to be inclusive for all incomes? What will you offer? Group therapy? Workshops? Mindfulness & Meditation? Art and creativity? Yoga? Being in nature? Pony trekking?

Breaking it down will take away the overwhelm as you start to see what steps need to be taken, what activities need to be done. It reminds you that you don't have to do it all now, you have time.

Be aware of any little voice in the back of your mind whispering that you couldn't possibly make this happen and check out chapter 7 on Imposter Syndrome if you hear it.

Have you heard of the Baader-Meinhof phenomenon? This phenomenon occurs when the thing you've just noticed, experienced or been told about suddenly crops up constantly, like if you've just bought a new red mini and you start seeing them everywhere you go. It gives you the feeling that out of nowhere, pretty much everyone and their cousin are talking about the subject. You're not crazy because yes, you're totally seeing it more, but of course, that's because you're noticing it more.

If your vision is top of mind, you'll naturally find opportunities opening up in your life: You'll see advertisements for retreats to check out and get inspiration from, notice possible venues, and possible activities. It will gain some momentum.

Let's do a little dreaming!

Now before you dismiss this as a waste of time, I urge you to keep an open mind about it because it is a highly effective way of moving forward. Goals are the things that keep us focused, and when we are focused, we get more done and achieve more success. So the last activity in this book is to do a little dreaming about how your life as a counsellor could be.

Activity: What could your life look like as a therapist?

Your personal vision statement is a written description of how you'd like your future to look. There is no right format or length; however, the more detailed and specific your vision is, the more connected to it you will be and the easier it will be to set your goals. Allow your mind to wander and really imagine how it would be to live your 'future' life. It doesn't matter if you don't know how to make it happen, just imagine a world where this is your norm.

- What would it feel like to wake up in the morning and know your day is going to be filled with doing the things that you feel passionately about?
- Allow yourself to think through how your day could be.
- Where will you be living? Will it be where you are now or somewhere else?
- What time do you get up?
- What do you see when you wake?
- What can you hear?
- What would your morning routine be like?
- Do you eat breakfast? Are you on your own, or sharing?

Turning Your Dreams Into Goals

- How do you feel?
- Do you go out to work or do you work from home?
- How does the transition from private life to work life feel?
- Imagine your perfect morning, what would that involve?
- What will you be doing?
- Now imagine taking your lunch break - what are you doing? Are you alone or with others? What do you eat and where? How does it taste, how does it smell?
- What would you like your perfect working afternoon to look like? See if you can imagine the details - what room will you be in? What style - light and airy, minimalist, cosy? What colours?
- What time will you finish work?
- How will you transition from work to leisure?
- What will your perfect evening routine look like? Will it involve relaxing or being active, being alone or in company?
- Who is in your life?
- What do you do for fun and for pleasure?
- How do you feel about being a therapist?

Try not to let your that reasonable, realistic voice limit you and play small, this is just a fun exercise looking at you, your wants and needs and future possibilities.

Re-visit this exercise often and add or remove things as you think of them. Defining what you want encourages you to focus, and the ability to focus will take you a very long way.

Your Growth Journal: Questions for reflection

- What do you want to create *for you*?
- What is your biggest dream, and how can you make that a reality?

CONCLUSION

Firstly, well done for getting to the end of this book. I have *a lot* of books on my bookshelf, many that I haven't read all the way to the end, so I want you to acknowledge this. Give yourself a pat on the back, and write in your Growth Journal how it feels to have finished reading this. Celebrating every success both big and small highlights them to you and stops them passing by unnoticed. The more you notice the successes you have, the more your confidence will grow.

The fact you bought and read this book tells me that you take your success as a counsellor seriously. You want to not only work with more clients to get the transformations they want and need but also run a successful business and earn more money to satisfy your own wants and needs. That is a balanced result.

I hope this book has inspired you to to take action, as it's actions that bring results. You may have doubts and fears, and that's normal, we all do but look at everything you've gone through in your life to get to this point. You are intelligent, compassionate and resilient, and you can totally do this.

The more action you take, the easier it gets. Every blog you write will improve, every social media post is an opportunity to learn. Being in private practice is a never-ending journey so stay curious, keep learning and enjoy the ride. Celebrate your wins, learn from your mistakes and most importantly, keep moving forward. Baby steps are fine, this isn't a race. You have time.

Your future is in your hands, and you have the power to make it whatever you want it to go. When you run into doubts, ask yourself 'What would I say to a client if they felt like this?'. Nurture your inner cheerleader to drown out the inner critic.

For me, finishing writing this book was hard, mainly due to my perfectionism. I wanted to tell you every little thing I could to help you with your private practice journey, but I couldn't, or I would have ended up with a whole encyclopedia of books! Each chapter, each subchapter could have been a book in itself, so I had to pare the information down to give you an overview of each of the subjects.

However, all the subjects are expanded on in the Grow Your Private Practice Club, so if you want more in-depth help with any or all of these subjects along with a supportive community of peers, then come and join us there. You will be very welcome.

All that's left to do is wish you all the very best for your future. I'm not going to wish you luck because it's not down to luck, you are in charge of your own success. Keep showing up consistently, doing the work and stay curious. Do what you enjoy and enjoy what you do, and you will find success.

However, I will wish you abundance and joy for a bright future.

With love, Jane xx

RESOURCES

Bibliography

Books and internet links

https://www.them.us/story/why-i-see-a-black-queer-therapist accessed 15/11/2019

Duffield Thomas, Denise. - https://luckybitch.com/be-a-contributor/

Kat Love. www.katlove.com

Hendricks, Gay. The Big Leap', HarperOne; 1 edition (15 May 2010)

Ash , Mary Kay The Mary Kay Way : Timeless Principles from America's Greatest Woman Entrepreneur. John Wiley & Sons (17 Jun. 2008)

Wheatus song 'Teenage Dirtbag' https://www.wheatus.com/ accessed 15/11/2019

ABOUT THE AUTHOR

Hi! I'm Jane Travis, and I'm the counsellor that helps other counsellors to grow their private practice.

We've all had our journeys to get to where we are now, and I've had my own struggles to fight through without support, and it's been hard. Often I've felt it's all just too much, have felt overwhelmed and doubted my abilities. All I needed was a little less criticism and a little more help. But I'm nothing if not tenacious and don't like being told I can't do something, so I've powered through.

When I see others going through the same struggles with insecurities and lack of confidence, I get frustrated because I know that all they need is a little support and encouragement to get them going. A little time to find that confidence and develop some skills.

Now I'm in a position where I help other counsellors that are struggling to build their practice. To offer encouragement, support, motivation and inspiration. I help them grow their self-confidence and belief in themselves, develop new skills and go on to have a practice that allows them freedom. Freedom to work in a way that feels right for them and with issues they feel passionate about. To work with creativity and create financial freedom. To have choices. To achieve their goals and dreams.

And most importantly, when someone criticises or tries to put them down they can think (or say!) 'I don't need your permission, so F*** you!'.

I decided to develop the Grow Your Private Practice Club because at the heart of who I am is a person who can't resist supporting others. I developed the club and then wrote this book so that I could reach as many counsellors as possible.

My aim in life is to support you to have the thriving practice that you deserve and to have a community that you feel safe in.

The Grow Your Private Practice Club is all about showing members how to grow their knowledge and skills while giving that vital support. This way, your inner strength grows and has a positive knock-on effect, so you find the courage to feel comfortable about marketing and confident in your abilities.

The Club provides training on all aspects of running a private practice, including practical aspects, like what to post on social media, and mindset issues, like how to handle self-sabotage. We have monthly planning meetings, guest experts, member-only discounts, courses, workshops and resources. We also have an active community of members all looking to connect, support and be supported by their peers.

I created this club to guide counsellors that are struggling to take control of their practice. To take away the overwhelm, to save time and to give clarity, and it's priced to help people at all stages of their journey. So please, don't battle on alone, it's just not necessary. Come and join us, and grow your confidence as well as your practice. You will be very welcome.

In my spare time, I walk my gorgeous dog Kimmy and eat Maltesers...

Printed in Great Britain
by Amazon